SECRETS FROM
THE STREET

Just In Time Press

6118 Hupa Road
Sarasota, FL 34241.
wnjrdbajit@ij.net

ISBN : 978 - 0 - 615 - 39770 - 2
Library of Congress Control Number : 2010935706
Secrets From The Street / Walter Nussbaum Jr.

Cover design by Ron Sanders
Page design by Randi Ball , OFD

Contact Walt through the website:
www.secretsfromthestreet.com
Bulk purchase information is available.

SECRETS FROM THE STREET

INDUSTRIAL AND COMMERCIAL BUSINESS-TO-BUSINESS SALES

Walter Nussbaum, Jr.

ACKNOWLEDGMENTS

My wife, Beverly Burger, deserves notable kudos for her participation in "*Secrets from the Street*". Beverly read and reread the manuscript from inception to finish. Her suggestions to add, or change particular parts made "Secrets" a better book, and her persistence that some subject matter be eliminated proved to be accurate. Beverly validated my writing skill with unwavering support. She was also instrumental in the publication of "Secrets from the Street".

Four other friends read "Secrets" in manuscript form and I want to acknowledge their input.

First, my son Frank Nussbaum. Previously in sales and now a schoolteacher, Frank highlighted parts of my book he particular liked, and suggested changes elsewhere. His opinion influenced several areas. It was Frank's idea that I devise a chart for Chapter Four.

Donna Vidas was an outside salesperson with a major distributing company. She added sensibility to "Secrets." She too empathized the value of certain parts and questioned others. Her editing contribution was especially helpful.

Dave Smith is a VP of Operations at a mid-size manufacturing company. His compliments were encouraging, particularly his suggestion that I stay true to my way of expression.

Buddy Sebastiao, the president at a large manufacturing company, read "Secrets" during its early raw stages. His positive assessment of my book's potential was welcome news, though I imagine he swallowed hard digesting some of its early distracting-digressions.

Thanks to you all, I'm VERY VERY grateful that you took time to read, edit, and offer suggestions for my book.

Thanks too, to my professional editor Joyce Standish. Her superb editing fit perfectly with my writing style. Her comment that I had written a "real winner," confirmed my decision to publish.

TABLE OF CONTENTS

During my sales career I've experienced jubilation, gratification, and success. There's also been frustration, humiliation, and anger. Then, there's MONEY, which is its own reward or conundrum. Even lasting friendships can develop. If you're good, you'll make enemies too, but they're soon forgotten.

Walter Nussbaum, Jr.

INTRODUCTION

© 'SECRETS FROM THE STREET'

Mix years of outside sales street smarts with liberal portions of philosophical wit, recycle into 50,000 words, and you have *Secrets From The Street*: A **window** for aspiring buisiness salespeople to **preview their potential** in the world of Industrial and Commercial Business-to-Business Sales (ICBBS). Devoid of glitz, canned speeches, and unreal expectations, this book provides the tools to master the secrets of outside business sales. *Secrets From The Street* is not a motivational discourse; it reveals on-the-job, and in-your-face experiences. My *Secrets* ascribe to a theory of outside sales that I call "prosperity with dignity."

Secrets gives the means to become innovative and convincing through a creative process I garnered from years of experimentation. A degree or technical background are not prerequisites. One chapter details a step-by-step, day-by-day approach to initiate sales from your own research. You'll learn a unique procedure for telephone calls and sales visits with examples of technique.

To re-light the fire of those with prior sales history my methods add new strategy, opening untraveled avenues to explore. Individuals who consider themselves shy can purge such self-imposed images, and have a fulfilling career in ICBBS. I'll show you how! For someone who thrives on challenges, ICBBS offers a wide open opportunity to create the future you've envisioned. However, understand clearly, a formula for effort is not included in these pages.

If the contents of my book don't excite you, or if you find it intimidating, forget outside sales and save years of exasperation. On the other hand, if you're not dissuaded by the most difficult experiences I relate, you've got IT—the spirit to find a way to make the sale.

I will promise this. After reading this material, you'll know if being an outside ICBBS salesperson offers the opportunity and rewards you're seeking. You may not always agree with my philosophy that slips into these pages now and then, but if it makes you think, gets your attention, that is, after all, what selling is all about.

Everything manufacturers don't already know is here too. *Secrets From The Street* provides management with fresh insight into the everyday reality that business to business outside salespeople encounter. My book provides direction to sales managers enabling them to separate frustration from complacency among salespeople—a hard to distinguish line—allowing managers to foster salespeople with potential. The ground rules are not self-evident. My ethical approach is essential for success, and you'll discover why anything less will self-destruct.

The last chapter, *On Being A Manufacturers' Agent*, is for salespeople considering the jump to becoming a manufacturers' agent. I've also included a special supplement, *Take A Manufacturers' Agent To Market*, for manufacturers wishing to utilize manufacturers' agents to sell their products.

SECRETS FROM THE STREET

CHAPTER 1

THE ROBOT OR YOU

let's not become emotional about this

Is there a future for business-to-business salespeople that offers ongoing income growth potential? Some say manufacturing won't need business salespeople in ensuing years, when it's commonplace for manufacturers to bid on or find required materials via the Internet. Robots will eliminate emotional error, ego-biased decisions, discrimination, and human neglect, it's argued. In fact, robots (mobile computers) will soon walk, talk, carry a briefcase, and take clients to lunch. Settled, no need to read further. Robots will take over, you may as well put this book back on the shelf.

What follows will extricate the reader from such delusions.

Remember the early computer enthusiasts who proclaimed websites would replace salespeople? That's tantamount to the type of archaic predictions made for the telephone and later the fax machine. Now, *websites are no longer an advantage; they are a requirement.* Manufacturers' and distributors' websites with on-line ordering availability have become just another necessary tool for the salesperson.

Robots with human tendencies and intuitiveness aren't practical, except as novelties or to solicit grants for their designers. They can't replace business salespeople, particularly ICBBS salespeople. (Industrial and Commercial Business-to-Business Sales)

It's true, of course, that computer-controlled production processes do improve products, and that's as it should be. The U.S. Government's procurement entities list required materials on the Internet, allowing approved sources the opportunity to quote. Some high volume commodity manufacturers list their product availability for open bid over the Internet.

Mostly, however, competing companies, both large and small, equipped with today's latest electronic sales tools, offer various products and services, while continuing to compete on level playing fields. And, yes! It's once again the outside salesperson that makes the definitive difference. Face-to-face presentations that project confidence, the real thing, not rehearsed monologue; that's the essence of selling.

The following scenarios illustrate why ICBBS will offer exciting, well-paid careers for decades to come. What would occur if human outside salespeople were taken out of the sales loop and computers, (robots) handled sales transactions? A filing system, bearings, cleaning materials, or a sundry of items could be involved. Perhaps a robot purchasing agent, (we'll call him Horatio), needs products to maintain his company's production schedule. Here we introduce the robot salesperson (I've named her Clementine). Let's say she rolls into Horatio's office and offers a new widget or an equal that sells for less.

Horatio is struck with the beauty of her sleek plastic design. But is Clementine's widget actually competitive? Has her company been in business long enough to establish a track record for quality and on-time shipments? "No problem," it's argued, "Robots with the appropriate software can decide those things."

Would a design change or an update in Horatio's product be needed to use Clementine's less-expensive materials? Would they perform as well? What if the present vendor had made a slight change to a part, but kept the details to themselves? Neither Horatio nor his engineering group could advise Clementine to have her company do likewise, since Horatio's drawings weren't updated to reflect the change. A mistake by the present vendor? Usually not, because it happens frequently, an oversight on purpose. A salesperson can locate an engineer or construction foreman to verify drawings and even manually check a part; computers can't.

Horatio's engineering department must approve Clementine's new product or it could require a maintenance or construction foreman's okay. Would any one of them reject a new product because they're technically unqualified to make a comparison, then to avoid being discovered as incompetent, turn it down? You better believe it. Clementine would accept their rejection without question, turn, and roll out the door. Not so for the human salesperson who searches for reasons.

Let's take a look into the future. Horatio's company loses market share because new technology passed them by. The same electronics Clementine was trying to sell them. Too late, Horatio should have introduced Clementine and her new computer software to the proper person in his company. Unfortunately, Horatio didn't have a FEEL for it and couldn't find a way through his company's assorted hierarchy to a decision-maker or someone who'd interrupt their day and listen to Clementine's proposal.

Horatio is blamed. "You're fired," he's told. However, a brilliant resume within his hard drive lands him a purchasing position with a large general contractor. On Horatio's first day less-expensive construction parts are proposed on the Internet, and his new high powered chip orders them. Poor Horatio, onsite human workers aren't experienced with the new material and can't get it installed properly. Construction is delayed while a subcontractor who knows the product is brought in, only to find they don't employ the proper number of minority workers and the job is stalemated. Without a salesperson's involvement, Horatio clicked his way into trouble.

Imagine an attempt to program the preceding information into Horatio and Clementine. Smoke would filter from their square heads, as they slip into a deep lockup, never more to print again.

I would be the first to advocate changes to increase efficiency. My experiences with human ego creating errors has been, well, exasperating, to say the least. However, human salespeople are fixers, the front line, the cutting edge that slips in, hammers home, dredges up, explains how, pushes through, and generally gets it done.

Let's revisit similar situations using a salesperson.

Salespeople must sometimes bypass purchasing, then ascertain who controls final decisions on the product they're selling. It could be an engineer, a sales person, a maintenance person, a construction foreman, owner, or plant manager.

Case in point. Within OEM (Original Equipment Manufacturer) sales I've discovered many unlikely candidates that were decision-makers. In one instance, I knew a mechanical design engineer, who, for complicated internal reasons within his company, rejected the offer to become chief design engineer. However, I went to him, when the electrical engineer, who preferred the status quo, my competitor, quit. The new electrical design engineer soon recognized the company's political flavoring and followed the advice of the mechanical engineer, designing my improved electrical product for use in a new machine they manufactured. Only I knew the mechanical engineer's influence would affect the new electrical design engineer's decision; it was a human thing.

Back with Horatio. With a repaired hard drive he manages to get another purchasing job. Through the Internet bidding process he again finds Clementine's company, but is distracted when he opens a link to her personal website, and Horatio fails to order Clementine's parts on time.

Human relationships make a difference. In this case, Horatio needs Clementine to convince management within her company to make adjustments in their manufacturing schedule and thereby provide Horatio's shipments when he needed them. But, and this is a big BUT, profits were marginal. Clementine got the new order on price, but her delivery promise didn't include changes to her company's production schedule. Her manager's loyalty rested with established, more profitable customers also waiting for deliveries. Sentiment (human loyalty) in business is a good thing. Horatio's company production is stymied by the late delivery, and he's fired again. Finally, he deletes Clementine from his bookmark and heads for the robot unemployment line. Salespeople with street smarts balance pricing with profitability, assuring their company can afford to bend for customers in special circumstances.

New, developing Internet software can help control cost and delivery schedules by taking advantage of international inventory and pricing. That purchase program is best served for specific commodity requirements. Some large retail outlets are perfecting the system, coercing their vendors into alliances. Yet, reason is in the head of the human beholder. Convincing decision-makers to select products or services; from a fork lift truck or a can of paint, to a machining service, requires the instincts of human outside salespeople, not just conclusions derived from word based software. The best sensors and software can't relate to some of the strange behavior we humans perpetuate. Instinct will always separate us from robots.

During my sales career I've experienced jubilation, gratification, and success. There's also been frustration, humiliation, and anger. Then, there's MONEY, which is its own reward or conundrum. Even lasting friendships can develop. If you're good, you'll make enemies too, but they're soon forgotten.

By now you will have concluded that ICBBS salespeople will be needed well into the future. If business-to-business sales is a new adventure or you're sales savvy, but still chasing your rainbow's end, a solution to reaching your goal is within these pages. Even the shy, can put aside their tentative nature and become good salespeople, maybe even great.

In time, self-learning super computers will enhance life's experience, creating a partnership, where we learn from each other. The experienced, streetwise, outside salesperson of the next century will still be there, developing sales, much like the magician producing illusions. How'd they do that?

"Is there a single secret to successful selling?" I've been asked.

Perception, perseverance and product knowledge are important. However, everyone knows *something different sells,* and the best way to ensure that advantage is to be yourself.

Let's get started.

CHAPTER 2

PURCHASING, FUN AND GAMBLES

don't slip on the bull ####,
you may become permanently stuck

Individuals who purchase materials to be used by the companies where they're employed constitute "Purchasing Departments." This group is defined by several names, whose titles continue to evolve. Most familiar are PA's, (Purchasing Agents), Purchasing Managers, Buyers, Material Managers, Planners, Commodity Managers, and on and on. Owners and/or general managers of small companies purchase, but do so under different circumstances because they answer to no one. Some might say that Chapter Two isn't in the proper sequence, that an introduction to selling for the first time might be more appropriate. However, knowing about the pitcher's tendencies before you step to the plate will get you a hit.

This section could be a book on its own entitled *Dealing with Purchasing Departments* or *How to Maintain Your Dignity When the Going Gets Tough.*

It's appropriate to begin the purchasing chapter with a joke, and that's not a pun. My favorite sales cartoon depicts a salesman's failed attempt to see a buyer, even when his product is exactly what the customer needs. That situation has confounded salespeople through the ages. The lesson is worth the digression, so picture this scene.

It's medieval times. A grand castle is built on top of a rise encompassed by expansive fields of colorful wild flowers. Sir Beyer, Lord of Ego Castle, is standing on the castle wall in full uniform surveying his valley. Though his armor and pointed metal headdress weigh him down, he remains undaunted and determined to defend his domain. As the sun rises over the treetops, the last haze of morning fog lifts to reveal his enemy, a Roman army of 10,000 men advancing toward Sir Beyer's castle. Inside the walls the castle guard, 500 strong, stand ready, their long spears reaching skyward. Even though vastly outnumbered, they're prepared to charge across the mote to meet the onslaught of the Roman army. Silently they wait, anticipating Sir Beyer's signal to open the gate.

Suddenly, two of Sir Beyer's servants attempt to interrupt his concentration.

"There's a salesman here to see you sir, it's very important you talk to him," he says.

"Salesman! Now! Send him away I don't have time for a salesman," he answers in a demeaning tone.

In the distance the Roman army continues its approach. The front lines begin moving faster, pointing their spears forward, their confidence growing, as they march closer.

"Sir Beyer, perhaps you should see this salesman," his servants persists frantically. "He says he's come a long way and has a great product that can change your day. He says it's exactly what you need."

"No, I can't be bothered seeing some crazy salesman," he says, waving them off. "Can't you see that we've got a battle to fight?"

Sir Beyer, his armor clanging with every step, heads down the stone stairway to join his army. With much fanfare he orders the mote gate opened. The determined salesman springs up the back steps of the wall attempting to catch Sir Beyer. He's too late. At the top he sees the advancing Roman army.

"Yikes!" the salesman cries and hurriedly retreats to his waiting wagon, quickly covers the 50-CALIBER MACHINE-GUN he had to sell, then urges his horses onward "Get me the hell out'a here!" *"PUFF"* he disappears in a cloud, back to the future.

Before writing another word, I must say, like most situations, there's promise where at first glance one sees complications. Dedicated buyers exist in a very complex world of purchasing, and they are often asked to do the impossible. They sort through countless hours of paperwork, and yet are expected to see salespeople in their spare time, and then, with some degree of enthusiasm, pass on their products to responsible people within their companies. They're also responsible for investigating the feasibility of new widgets, when the price is enticing. Purchasing people become scapegoats for other department errors, whose failure to give purchasing adequate time or information creates late delivery or production mistakes. Some of these short-comings present an opportunity a salesperson can use to assist a buyer and get them out of harm's way.

An aggressive and creative sales initiative is a must. Such initiative includes going to bat for buyers, even battling their own company hierarchy to speed up delivery, or accept an order change at the last minute, while maintaining the original delivery promise.

That type of dedicated assistance to a buyer is never forgotten.

Unfortunately, on the other hand, in some situations bypassing a buyer is essential, or your widget will remain "on hold," while your competitor finds a timely avenue to a decision-maker. We'll deal with that situation later.

When your customer's purchasing department demonstrates that they realize your company deserves a reasonable profit to be proficient, you've got a valued customer. Unfortunately, I think there are some PA's, decision-makers, or managers that don't have the foresight to recognize driving down their vendors' profits can lead to disaster for themselves down the road. A good marriage means both parties profit, that both parties foresee the vendor arrangement as long-lasting, that both parties expect an equitable arrangement.

Seasoned salespeople may say, "Yeah, I know all about purchasing department problems. Why drag it out in a special chapter?" Because even with my approach and experience, I've missed the boat calling on the wrong PA and unknowingly wasted TIME. And TIME is everything to an outside salesperson.

We've all experienced an abrupt doctor in the examining room, and it's obvious why: TIME IS MONEY. As often happens, it's best explained by example.

This scenario occurred 15 years back. A gear company I represented got an inquiry from another manufacturers' agent. This new agent had little gear or rep experience. He sent an RFQ (Request For Quote) with prints to my gear company not knowing or caring that they already had a representative—me—in the territory. He referred to the high volume and future potential of the part, even suggesting purchasing had given him inside info. To quote the job would take lots of engineering time. Now the interesting part. It so happened that this customer was already an account of mine and my gear company for all their gear needs, and we naturally recognized the gear prints and part numbers involved in the query. The gears in question were, in fact, being discontinued in lieu of a more sophisticated gear train. We had new prototype parts already in production. It was obvious this new salesperson was given an inquiry with no merit. The gears the purchasing department wanted the new salesperson to quote were being discontinued, a terrible, terrible waste of everyone's time.

How could such a thing happen? It could be the PA did not know the gear was being discontinued, having little communication with his engineering group or marketing department; believe me, that's commonplace, and in that case the PA's blameless. Uncommon, but conceivable in slow times, the PA needed to generate work for his department. In time you'll learn to recognize the signs, and that's essential to survive as an outside salesperson.

A few more PA comments. The next situation is tricky. You have lunch with the buyer—anyone for that matter—whose responsibility includes buying, and the following occurs. He openly relates his problems at work in an attempt to get your empathy. More disarming, he expects your response, while mentioning politics or philosophy you find distasteful. It's best to simply suggest that you've heard similar comments from others. They still do not know you disagree, and better still, without your part of that game, you'll get back to business sooner. In other words, don't get involved in disruptive social or other controversial discussions with a customer or DPB (Definite Possibility of Business). They'll forget you didn't participate, but will remember if you disagree. Don't dismiss the previous encounter; it is one of the important lessons in this book.

If you had to go around purchasing to procure a PO (Purchase Order), but must later deal with them on delivery schedules or other needs, be courteous. Don't ever, ever, gloat.

Remember, purchasing often buys by part numbers, if you're selling widgets, they may say they don't use them. If, because of the products they manufacture, you know they must buy widgets, ask if they recognize the name of one of your competitors and go from there.

Some purchasing people have no intention of ever buying from you, but hold your interest, enabling them to use your pricing to keep their vendors, your competition, in line. They're doing their job at your expense. It's time we all waste. Continuing with them depends on the overall potential and your judgment. You might get their business if a screw-up occurs with their present source. So, if value exists, be diligent, quote and stay in touch, but be aware of the potential waste of time. It's often a good idea to relate your quoting doubts to your management, giving them an opportunity to be involved in the decision to quote or not to quote.

Purchasing management in large corporations require a different approach; they can control purchases, yet must adhere to strict preset policies. Each situation has different subtleties. Here's a tip that also fits in the sales chapter: If you're getting nowhere, try for purchasing management. A manager may pass you on to the buyer who is responsible for ordering your widgets. However, if your type of widget is presently a pressing matter, they'll likely get involved themselves.

Some buyers who purchase parts for resale are also re-quoting your product. These people are keenly interested in the best source available as their customer is their responsibility.

We'll deal with the first sales contact in depth in the sales chapter, but, avoid seeing the PA on initial contact when you already know someone else in the plant calls the shots. If you start with a PA, then later go over that PA's head; that's worse than going direct to the decision-maker first, then to the PA. It's less aggravating to the PA. I know, I've done it both ways.

An uncomfortable relationship with a buyer is like a bad marriage. Neither party says what they're really thinking but function together in a mood of subtle discontent. Unfortunately, as customers, you can't get divorced.

Competent PA's will give you a truthful response when they aren't the decision-makers. They might explain that their time's limited, and price won't move them, unless there's a significant difference. Don't give up with competent buyers, they represent a chance in the future. Oftentimes a new widget can get their attention immediately, and they'll suggest you see someone else, even calling them to ask if they have time to see you. I've had the pleasure of dealing with such PA's, both women and men; they're respected by their fellow employees and salespeople. With this kind of PA it's your product and presentation that matter.

A comment: Acronyms are used throughout the book to learn terms, and procedures. Don't worry if you don't remember them; they're defined on page 216.

CHAPTER 3

SCARED TO LIFE

outside sales can jump-start your battery

It's been said that outside sales is no place for the timid. I disagree. In fact, those types usually approach the job with an open mind. So if timid fits your demeanor, keep reading. We'll put that part of your personality to good use. It's true that the first sales visit of your life can make your heart beat faster than a five mile run or watching your 50 to 1 long shot at the race track pull two lengths ahead in the stretch. If you're so laid back that nothing bothers you, not even making your first sales call on a PA that's having a bad day because his boss chewed him out for late deliveries of your product, then skip this chapter. Seasoned salespeople reading my book may be tempted to do just that, but don't. The information will serve as a good wake-up call.

With new salespeople there's another matter needing attention. *Webster's Dictionary* defines "motivate" as: To provide with a motive. Well, *MONEY* is the sales person's incentive. *You won't find any motivation in this book.* Creative artists like Vincent Van Gogh worked with no monetary reward. He sold only one painting during his lifetime. His reward was a window into the meaning of life and the satisfaction to interpret what he saw. I've read he literally starved himself into insanity. Sales requires similar dedication, but certainly not the same ending. Let's be realistic; in the working world money motivates. If it's not enough to move you then please forget selling as a career. Selling's an art, and some of the best highs I've experienced came from successes in the sales profession. I'm certainly thankful for the creative genius of Van Gogh, and if you possess such talents, please use that avenue of expression, so we can all enjoy your work.

In my opinion the hypothesis of motivation, defined in *Webster's Dictionary* as, "A force of influence," has been gravely abused. Ask yourself: How do some of the most prolific sales entrepreneurs create wealth? We're all aware of the billions of dollars made in the weight-loss industry. The same is true for cosmetic and beautification enterprises that motivate by promising a transformation. There's another, and it, too, is about changing people, except it alters the mind. No, not drugs. I'm referring to the *MOTIVATION BUSINESS*.

This conviction won't be popular with my colleagues in the sales business, who've attached themselves to that bandwagon. Motivation has been diminished by its exploitation. I recognize that some of the most respected public figures are popular speakers. Many religious orators have a special talent to stir a congregation, and some have become quite famous. Unfortunately a few made headlines for all the wrong reasons. However, admittedly, talented speakers can motivate.

At this juncture I want to **differentiate** my concept of **inspiration** from the **motivation** comments that follow. Speaking (language), is not the basis for inspiration as it is for motivation, *ACTIONS ARE*: Courage in the face of difficult circumstances; our military; giving of oneself for the benefit of others in spite of personal sacrifices; the handicapped that carry on without quitting; the aged that fight through each day. And how about those stories of animals whose courage astounds us? Those are but a few inspiring examples and thankfully there's a long list. Inspiration affects everyone it touches while also serving—sometimes unwanted—as reminders of where we fall short. Everyone has the opportunity to make a difference during their lifetime. And yes, inspiration by the fact that it's all around you can permanently energize the distraught salesperson. Music inspires too, try it.

Motivational career speakers can be entertaining, but when it impacts sales personnel, their remarks need close scrutiny. Alas, we know talented political speakers often win elections regardless of the facts.

Motivation has its place. Being fired-up is often beneficial, and it feels good being part of something. Yet, like *BLACK COFFEE,* it's only temporary; motivational speakers don't warn us about that. Too often, when the caffeine wears off, the salesperson's lost, and before it can be prevented, they're depressed and ineffective, or worse, quit without looking back to understand what went wrong. "How could that buyer have been so rude?" they ask. "I can't take another rejection," they tell themselves. "I had the best product and price. Why did she buy from my competition?" or often, "I can't find anyone interested."

Every individual's ideology is different, and prepared motivational jargon is quickly lost with the everyday conflicts salespeople face on the street. Take that to the bank.

As a manufacturers' agent my motivation was money, and yes, for me, the excitement of the chase. Money's the ultimate reason we work. If shooting for lots of it doesn't excite you, then sales isn't your calling.

Let's face it: Outside salespeople are manipulators, experts at convincing others to believe as they do about their products or services. *Webster's Dictionary* offers this definition for manipulation: "To change by artful or unfair means so as to serve one's own purpose." Drop the word "unfair," and we've realistically defined an honest professional outside salesperson, and that's the crux of it. An ICBBS salesperson intends to change a customer's thinking, and their purpose is to make money. Motivation doesn't fit that description. *Outside salespeople spawn believers, not followers.* Salespeople should be convinced about the value of what they're selling or switch and sell some other widget.

High-pressure motivational speakers do the most damage. Seminars that convince the newcomer to sell for organizations whose products are stagnant, or less than legitimate, borderline, or without merit, give outside sales a bad name. Much worse, bad experiences destroy the confidence of those considering the profession for the first time, and too often deters those who did have a talent for selling. What a waste!

Once the BLACK COFFEE's worn off, you'll need determination that comes from within. Motivation fades with hard knocks and doesn't beget hard work over the long haul. The need to pay your mortgage must suffice to carry you forward. I don't advocate the end of speakers at sales meetings. I've spoken at sales seminars myself. Entertaining remarks while explaining product advantages, or actual "how to" sales procedures, is time well-spent. It's the misleading, self-serving motivators that really irk me.

Persistence is a key. Those new to the sales profession and slow off the block need not despair, if others are initially more successful. Newcomers need to understand that persistence, learning new techniques, and getting over the early hurdles, actually serve to give them stamina for the future. I've had that experience. Each success, no matter how small or how difficult to achieve, is a tonic for shyness. Confidence grows and instills personal self-understanding. "Self" is a strong word in this context. It's a difficult place to reach, but one's life progress depends on it; others can't give it to you, or take it away.

It's a fact that being an outside salesperson's a demanding career. It's not some regimented desk job we're talking about. Your mind and will are challenged daily. The feeling of accomplishment is gratifying, natural, and doesn't require motivation to make it poignant.

There must be a balance. If money and self-respect gained from developing business and loyal customers isn't enough to offset disappointment or encounters with difficult buyers, then don't try being a salesperson. It's part of the lifestyle. Then again, anyone who allows actions or opinions of others to affect their self-esteem, has a problem regardless of their occupation.

I have made sales visits and traveled with countless numbers of sales people, new and experienced, during my career. I knew if they had "it" within the first hour. The tools are in the pages of this book; you have only to assimilate them: Assertive, Determined, Creative, Disciplined, Honesty, Imagination, Persistence, Self-confidence (know your product) and Strength. Notice that none of the conditions eliminate the timid personality, nor do they require college degrees.

I'll probably repeat this many times: "Don't become a salesperson, if you're looking for a free ride." Find another job, please, something easier. Hide in a closet or behind a desk in a large corporation. I know some people try for the easy ride in sales, but it always costs everyone money, themselves included. Those types that I call "bozos," can confuse the issue early, since all salespeople take time to develop. It's the bozo's fault that managers initiated cumbersome, formulated, outside sales reports, and other sales checks that have little value other than to record times and dates of sales visits. The old adage "Time Will Tell," eventually gets rid of the bad apples in sales, but surely drags down efficiency. Managers, on the other hand, must give new salespeople "Time" to persist, to overcome hurdles that new people encounter.

If you don't want to be burdened with sales reports, forecasts and other paperwork your company will likely require, become an independent manufacturers' agent. First, you have to be crazy, along with all the other attributes I mentioned. In addition, there'll be no salary, no expenses, no car, no insurance, nothing but you; and you'll need a living expense investment. Everything you need to know about being a manufacturers' agent is in Chapter Twelve.

If you're sufficiently skeptical about a career in sales, let's move on to the first sales call and dispel misunderstandings. Those who enjoy meeting people will have an easier time with the pressure of that first sales visit. Others who don't feel particularly comfortable around new people can make it through the first weeks okay and go on to become successful.

You probably sell every day. You and your spouse give reasonable reasons to the other as to why you want to see a particular movie, buy a TV, purchase a car. You communicate your thinking, your values, your perception why one thing is better than another. If you disagree, you weigh positives against negatives. After all, you sold your spouse on your positive traits.

If you're new to sales or uncertain of yourself, listen up. Here's how creativity and preparation play a major role in selling. Let's say the husband wants a new TV, giant size with full surround sound. He knows his wife wants to use that money for a new sofa, designer style, with a big price tag. He plans his preparation for the forthcoming conversation. He has all the advantages thought through and has some idea what he expects his wife will say about the sofa.

"We don't need a new TV. Besides that monstrosity will ruin the ambiance of the room."

"But we both watch TV," he plans to counter. "The investment's for both of us, and I never sit on the sofa. If we spend that kind of money, it should be for both of us."

The husband pictures the encounter in his mind. That'll never work, he says to himself, then begins to create another image, think of better words that will SELL his wife.

So, for you salespeople with big butterflies about a first sales encounter, imagine how you'd try talking your better half into something you want, something that you know darn well your mate doesn't. And here's an important aspect: You're convinced they'll appreciate the value of your conviction in the end. Hold that picture. Now think of the buyer, be as relaxed with that person as with your spouse. Conjuring that image may be a little daunting, depending on the buyers physique, but do it. Just before you walk into the buyer's office or approach their desk, conjure up that scene. Think how at ease you are, how confident you feel about convincing your better half of what you want, of the advantages of it. It's similar to an athletic endeavor, where you picture yourself making the perfect swing in tennis or golf, or the hit-saving catch in softball. This buyer, you're about to see isn't any better, any smarter, than your better half. I guarantee it! Therefore, you have no reason to be afraid. Just sell 'em; it works and it definitely relaxes one before and during the sales visit.

Don't ever have an alcoholic drink before a sales visit. You might think it relaxes you, but it stifles creativity, and even worse, eliminates quick thinking. That's another of the best tips in this book: if you get caught up in that habit, it's over before you begin.

Like so many things in life, those people that overcome some difficulty, some hurdle, like butterflies or anxiety grow in strength and often achieve more than others who have an easier path.

There's a difference in selling your spouse and selling a buyer. When you talk to your spouse, live-in friend, life partner, to have them see your way about something; you're certainly talking to the right person. No doubt about them being instrumental in having a say in the decision. Regrettably, in business one can't presuppose the person you're trying to convince has anything to do with decision-making, even if that's their title, even if they imply they do, even if they *say* they do. Finding the decision-maker is one of the main exercises in this book, and details follow in Chapter Four.

More information for new salespeople. Don't, don't, ever use canned spiels when selling. I don't care how well they're polished, how new and ingenious the author says they are, don't use them. Remember, the buyer hears that stuff every day. No matter how different they might seem to their creator, canned speeches are all the same. Every individual who reads the same instruction is taking the same approach. You're dealing with intelligent people, and they're insulted by canned comments. During election years I've heard, "Let's move forward together," expressed so many different ways, in so many different tones, in so many varying degrees of enthusiasm by some politician, that I realize how limited human speech really is.

Have you had a salesperson use this one with you? It's been around awhile. "You're a real challenge Mr./ Mrs. So-and-So." A lawn mower salesman whom I was questioning about price comparisons used those words on me. I suppose for those folks who seldom have encounters with professional salespeople, that old gimmick can be effective. Its purpose is to imply some sort of personal connection, some kinship between the salesperson and the customer. That lawn mower salesman meant me to believe he recognized me as special, and therefore intended for me to believe he was different from his competition. I'll repeat this often: THE ONLY POSITIVE WAY TO BE DIFFERENT IS TO BE YOURSELF.

So again, repetitive canned sales pitches turn off buyers. The next comment is very important. **When you approach a client put yourself on their level.** Be courteous but not gushing.

Appearance? It goes without saying, one should dress professionally.

Selling should have nothing to do with being male or female, tall or short, overweight or skinny, old or young, beautiful, or handsome, but you can bet your life it does. Some male PA's definitely favor a young, attractive woman, and the same goes for female PA's and handsome men. I remember an instance when visiting an engineer about gears—a woman who could've been a top fashion model—walked past me leaving his office. I discovered she was a mechanical engineer and a competitor. Since I knew the engineer, I surmised correctly my potential account walked out the door with the model. Another interesting area is the natural affiliation of age. A 25-year-old PA, engineer, or construction foreman is likely to favor a 25-year-old outside salesperson over an older person, all other things being equal. However, if you've successfully reached the decision-maker, *knowing your product* is a leading factor; it makes all the difference, even if your competition stepped out of a fashion magazine.

Be pleasant to the receptionist. This group can be a kick. I've met some receptionists who remembered my name after a few visits and who were always helpful and proficient. And they're to be appreciated. Then there are those you're sure worked as a prison guard before being a company receptionist. "Ghoul" is the first word that comes to mind, when I think of one particular receptionist I encountered. When I checked Webster, it read: a legendary evil being that robs graves and feeds on corpses. That sounded a bit overstated, but then I remembered how her teeth seemed to protrude through a plastic smile, every time she squawked, "He's in a meeting and can't see you now." She always mispronouncing my name so badly I didn't recognize it. Anyway, the "ghoul" word remains for her.

You'll likely encounter your first potential customer in an office or maybe at their desk, or in a cubicle, a conference room, or at a construction building site. Start with "good morning" or "good afternoon." Don't start a greeting with "Madam" or "Sir". Later is okay, like with "Yes mam, it's shipping on time." Why not the "Sir" with a greeting? Remember what I said: Never talk up to anyone in business, naturally not down, but not up, either. It doesn't matter if you're 20 years old and the customer is 85. In outside sales *put communication on equal footing,* regardless if it's the company president or the janitor. I'm not implying disrespect, but just be relaxed. Like the husband and wife surround sound TV discussion, one gets nowhere speaking with disrespect **or** begging. The point being that with an equals approach, you present yourself as a self-confident professional.

Laid-back is better than pressure, but somewhere in between is more likely to get the order. You're there to sell, and they know it. Don't pretend that your visit's anything else. Friendly, fine, but get to business. There may be purchasing people who prefer salespeople who humble themselves, but don't do it. You'll feel dejected and irritable. Confidence projects a strong sales image, and after all, this is supposed to be a rewarding career, spiritually and financially. You can't accomplish either by belittling yourself.

What follows is not canned, but a suggestion for the new recruit, a starting place, an approach you can expand. It'll help with your first presentations. Try your own variation.

"My name's Happy Salesperson. I'm new at this, just in case you didn't notice (a standard phrase, and though it won't bother anyone, adjust it to suit). However, my product has a proven track record, (or is new or different) and I know it very well. All I need is your attention for a few minutes." If your butterflies cause you to stumble, you could add, "I wasn't expecting to be quite so anxious about this visit, *SO, JUST BLOCK ME OUT AND FOCUS ON THE PRODUCT.*" (They don't hear that often, but vary it anyway). This advice should give you some ideas to consider. A straightforward approach on a first time visit can leave a permanent good impression, and I know it works.

This is the best place to mention what I believe is a sales visit phenomenon, and can be a shock to new salespeople and can reoccur at the same place. However, being prepared will ease the pain. You leave a sales visit feeling gratified. The buyer liked your product. "Your widget could be a fix for an existing problem," he said. "I'll talk to maintenance about it, then arrange for you to see them. Give me a call next week or just drop by on Monday. I think there may be several widgets needed."

You feel great, the excitement I call the "Big Lift," keeps you going strong all week. Then you go by on Monday.

"He can't see you today," the receptionist says. Oh no! It's Ms. Ghoul! A sheepish grin gives away the delight she has in creating disappointment.

"You didn't mention my company name," you insist. "Tell him who I'm with. I know he wants to see me."

Your tone tells her you're going to be persistent, so she calls the PA again. A few words are exchanged. Her face lights up and almost giggling with delight, her words sounding like the chords of a song, sings, "Busy all this week. He said to try next week."

You leave, heading for the office to quit, never again to sell, then remember your mortgage. The next week the PA agrees to see you. He's in an okay mood, but has NO MEMORY of his interest in your widget and sees no reason why there would be. Flabbergasted, you sit in your car trying to understand what happened. Strength, you'll definitely need it here. Don't waste your time. Go on to the next visit. Several things may have occurred, the worst being he wanted to be disagreeable. Notice I said, "he." It's been my experience that women PA's don't pull this kind of stuff. Other stuff, yes, but usually not the deliberate things.

Most explanations for such an incident don't make sense, but it's usually a human thing. It may be simply that the PA was in a good mood the day of your previous visit. Maybe he got a raise or met a new girlfriend, and his enthusiasm carried over to your meeting. Unfortunately, later, he didn't remember you or what you said. However, another possibility exists: The PA may have been rejected by the maintenance department, when he made a presentation of your widget. If the maintenance foreman ridiculed the PA, because the problem was solved two years ago, you were set up to have that scorn passed on to you.

Such an encounter doesn't surprise seasoned salespeople, but can be a demoralizing experience for new people. Don't despair, there will be a big lift, the real thing, lots of them. Use the rejection. Trust me, like lifting weights, persistence will make you stronger, since it hurts less every time. Understand the behavior of the PA as that person's problem, the company's problem, having no reflection on who you are or your sales ability. The experience will serve to make you savvy. If you've continued reading and still feel positive, that's a good omen too. You've likely got the fortitude needed by an ICBBS salesperson.

Remember, product knowledge before you make that first sales visit is essential. Only then can your presentation be *professional,* and therefore convincing.

The elements within a sales encounter bring me to an interesting example of the *professional effect.* New salespeople pay close attention. We've all experienced the following. You're visiting a large mall in search of the right pair of shoes. You start with lunch at one end of the mall, near where you park. The salesperson at a store near the food court shows you several pairs that don't fit your description. That salesperson's either indifferent or confused about questions of style and durability. You encounter the same results in two other stores. Eventually, at the far end of the mall a shoe salesman who seems genuinely interested in helping you, persists until he finds a pair that fits the bill. You try them on—great fit, but the cost seems exorbitant. You depart, deciding to take a chance with another cheaper pair at the first store. This time in the window of the first store you notice the exact same expensive pair of shoes you liked. The salesperson at the first store had overlooked showing them to you. They look great in the window, and you decide they're worth the cost. You notice this price is marked a couple of dollars less than the store with the well-informed, helpful salesperson. Your car is just outside the exit near this store.

What would you do? For my part, without hesitation, I'd walk to the other end of the mall, pay a little more for the shoes, then return to the exit near my car. I think many people would do the same. Why? I believe it's the human factor. We appreciate product knowledge, *FEEL ASSURED BY IT*, maybe even grateful. Often the difference in salespeople is less distinguishable; maybe both salespeople had the same interest in our needs, were equally courteous. Yet, many of us would still walk the extra distance to buy from one salesperson over another, because one was more knowledgeable, and equally important, seemed to be himself. In short we were sold.

I'll repeat this lesson many times: If in your first meeting with a client you don't have product knowledge, you'll do irreparable damage to your credibility. *TAKE THAT TO THE BANK.*

There is one exception to the above rule. After a while you'll become proficient in your field, where you can sell a new product in which you're lacking knowledge, but your overall technical skills make it possible to initially "wing it." Distributor salespeople, with a conglomeration of products to sell, have the opportunity to be extra-impressive based on their strength of product knowledge. The shoe salesperson scenario applies times ten.

If circumstances lead to a lunch visit, don't insult someone by exaggerating your relationship. Sure, small talk's natural, but don't imply personal friendship as a way to get an order; it's unnatural and will come across that way. Actual interest in what your customer or DPB has to say is one thing, but faking friendship is insulting. Being trusted by customers and DPB's is the height of an outside salesperson's accomplishments. I've also made a few genuine friends from business contacts over the years, and "a few" just about describes it. I recognize that there are business relationships, some high-priced ones, with a pretense of personal friendship. Those relationships are one sided, and it's always obvious that if the business wasn't there, neither would be the friendship. I suppose I'm somewhat idealistic about this issue, but friendship implies a state of being comfortable with someone, being unafraid to be sincere about who you are. I realize those precepts come in degrees, but don't attempt to fake it. No one enjoys fakers, not those around them, or those involved with them, so why bother? Be yourself!

Something to avoid: As you begin making the rounds, you'll find "easy places," companies where you and the client have some sort of bond, a mutual interest of sorts, and you hit it off. Fine, if they are, or have the potential to become, a good customer. Too often when the outside salesperson's having a tough day, they're drawn to visiting an "easy place" customer, or a potential customer who has little economic value. It's easier to talk about current events, and shared interest than asking imposing questions, and pushing for names of decision-makers. These salespeople kid themselves into believing they're working. I call that WFS. (Water Fountain Syndrome). A person that continues making trips to the water fountain to avoid starting a dreaded report or working the phone to make Check Out calls. We'll get into Check Out calls in Chapter Four too.

Another bad habit: If you're repetitive with the spoken word, it's done and too late to take it back. And the worst part? You've been classified, maybe subconsciously, but classified nonetheless, as boring or even worse, tiring. Usually this habit repeats itself, and unless you overcome it, credibility is lost. Don't be pegged, "AMATEUR TALKING," because unlike amateur sports you don't have a minor league. You're in the big time with the first outside sales visit. There's money on the line immediately.

If being *you* includes boring, long dissertations unrelated to the business at hand, or for that matter any boring story, long or short, cut out that part of you. Unfortunately, it's difficult to tell someone they fall into that category. Maybe a wife or friend or parent can use an adult approach, explained in Chapter Five, and tell a person they're repetitive. Even then the habit's difficult to break.

I once traveled with a salesman who related so many boring stories throughout the day, I switched him off like the radio in my dash. I interrupted his rambling during a visit with a DPB. He was a nice sensitive person, with good product knowledge, but needed someone to set him straight. If this book had been published at the time, I would've given him a copy and marked this page. In retrospect I should have been blunt with him, as I am here. Think about your own habits. Can you detect yourself doing the same thing? Bite your lip, hold your breath. It's true that you may have to listen to a few boring stories from customers during lunch, but don't join in. Naturally, if it's an interesting topic, and you have something to offer, that's fine, but be quick. Don't drag it out. Humor's always nice in both directions, but keep it brief too.

One more thing about conversing with a DPB or others, and now I'll be blunt: *DON'T INTERRUPT.* That's it, plain and simple. I could take several paragraphs to expound on the negatives of this habit, but that would certainly be boring.

The *DISCIPLINE* feature of my formula to achieve your goal is essential. Following is typical example: Early in my career I was pushing hard to break even. Time was my enemy. For an independent manufacturers' rep without a salary, being persistent (discipline) is more than essential; it's survival. Late one afternoon, using my map/time guide, another feature in Chapter Four, I found myself looking for a parking place to make a sales visit with an engineer. I could rarely catch this guy on the phone. I had established his company as a DPB, and decided an unannounced visit was my best option.

It was 4:30 and raining hard. They were located in an older area of the city where parking places were at a minimum. Their small lot was full. I drove around the block several times, finally catching someone vacating a spot on the curb. When I finally presented myself and my briefcase soaking wet to the receptionist, it was 4:45. She was nice enough, suggesting, however, that it was unlikely the engineer would see me. She announced me correctly, and, *guided by my instruction, mentioned the type of product that was responsible for my visit.* There are instances when you should insist the receptionist describe your product in announcing your visit. We were both surprised, when the engineer invited me up to his office. *That wouldn't have happened, had the receptionist not announced my product along with my name. Remember that!* Push that point when you know about a specific requirement.

Details, Details. I was there two hours. It just so happened, their present source for AC (Alternating Current) electric motors came up short on special applications. Though I'm not a professional engineer, I know my products and was able to ask questions and record all the necessary parameters that he introduced. I was taken to the plant. He turned on the lights, and I saw their product and what was needed to overcome an engineering design fault. Now, talk about the "Big Lift." Imagine how that one felt, when I walked out their door. I was truly singing in the rain. A couple of days later with the assistance of my inside engineer, we had a proposal. That company became a good, long-standing customer, and there was even an extra bonus. I'd just become divorced, and so had he. We went to several singles hangouts together. And, oh yes, that was my seventh visit of the day. PERSISTENCE, PERSISTENCE.

Reader:

At this juncture skipping ahead to
Chapter 12 is optional for the reader
whose interest is being an independent
manufacturers agent.
Reading Chapter 12 first can make a subtle
difference interpreting the information
in Chapter 4.

Thank You,
Just In Time Press

Chapter 4

Boot Camp

the past is important because it led to the present;
the future is important when it becomes the present

Each new day is your challenge. Get it right today, now, don't depend on the future. When computers evolve to the point where self-learning hardware becomes commonplace, "time" will be another matter. The laws of physics may change. We'll likely see a new reality, something that defies today's logic, where past, present, and future do come together. I know it hasn't happened in the future yet, or my deceased Grandmother would've come back in time to visit me. We're in the present, NOW, so we'll address the fundamentals and learn to *effectively use time* for outside sales visits.

Here we have a dividing line: Salespeople working for small or mid-size companies must research and locate their own potential customers, and therefore, must understand all the basics in this Chapter Four.

On the other hand, where larger companies furnish all leads, contact names, and even arrange appointments for their salespeople, the Check Out system that follows may not be as essential; however, it's always impressive when salespeople seeking a job bring lead-development to the table. Learning to use manufacturer's directories or their CD's to research and find DPB's through my Check Out call system is an absolute necessity for salespeople on their own.

A lead created by a salesperson that evolves into a customer is impressive no matter the company size. In either case, the communication and record keeping strategy in this chapter are generic to all sales visits. Boot Camp will hone your skills, so regardless of the employer's products, the distributor's specialty, or the service offered, you'll be able to recognize what avenue to travel, before you hit the street. I want this information to be as easy to digest as possible. Some books bog down presenting instructional detail. I've done my best so that doesn't happen. However, what follows has some similarity to a textbook, so relax, then concentrate.

Written sales visit lists are basic, and will become your personal creative tool to excel in commercial and industrial sales. *Efficient planning strategies* that cultivate DPB's make all the difference in the world. Take golf as an example, not now, keep reading. If you want to develop your golf game to its fullest, *learning the essentials at the beginning* is a must. If my program becomes your practice from the get-go, unlike great golf, your scores will be big.

It's time to deal with numbers. "Simple mathematics" or "I know that" you might say after reading the following. Possibly, but there are statistics that stay hidden behind our avoidance of "hard work reality." *Percentages are the key;* they will separate success from frustration. Defined by Webster's dictionary: "A percentage is a share of winnings, a part of a whole expressed in hundreds."

Let's take a break, and explore the importance of another percentage. Try this numbers puzzle. Consider poker. What's the exact percentage possibility for catching an inside straight with only the last round of up cards, in a 5-card stud game, yet to be dealt and your filling card for the inside straight isn't face-up anywhere on the table? Let's say there are six players including you; three besides you still remain in the game; while two others folded after their first up-card. The pot's $44.00. There are 52 cards, less those dealt, so would the odds be twelve to one to catch the straight (4 cards to a suit), or is it 48 to one, or is either accurate, since 5 unknown hole cards were dealt the other players? The answer can be found near the end of this book. YOUR BEGINNING!

Now, what's the relevance of all that to sales? Let's say you're an accomplished, experienced outside salesperson, a 9 on a 10 scale. (Wow! that's good). After proper Check Out (screening) preparation we'll say you make a good DPB hit 8% of the time, while visiting a new company. I define a hit as confirming with a visit that a DPB is definite, and that company should have interest in your product. If you make 10 sales calls a week (it should be more), that's .8 DPB per week or 41.6 new DPB's per year; enough new potential business to prosper. On the other hand if you're a fairly new salesperson your DPB discovery may only be 3%. However with extra effort (determination and persistence) and using the sales visit strategy that comes next, you make 30 sales visits a week; that's .9 DPB or 46.8 DPB per year, a good start on success. No poker uncertainties here. Easy math will tell you the kind of business the experienced salesperson would generate using my strategy and making 30 or more visits a week. Remember, (Chapter Four), is dedicated to the efficient use of time.

So now we come to the crux of it, the often maligned, always tough part of outside selling: FINDING THE BUSINESS AND DEVELOPING IT. My written Check Out sales call (telephone) list and a list for sales visits follow.

If you've gotten tired or aren't in the mood for concentration, have an apple, or just hang it up for now, and mark this page. Avoid any semblance of WFS. I considered placing this chapter toward the end of the book, concerned that the nuts and bolts may be tiring and diminish interest in some of the more entertaining chapters to follow. However, it belongs here, so let this be your first new bit of persistence. To be sure Chapter Four is absorbed, I suggest reading it more than once. It might be best to read it fully the first time without stopping to analyze the details; do that on the second reading.

I remember having difficulty impressing the importance of written preparation while training outside salespeople. "Not necessary," they'd say. "Let's just get at it. Tell me how to approach the client. We can make up some sort of report as we go along." Too much detail they insisted. It may seem that way at first, but my method takes you to another level of efficiency, making your creativity more useful. Important decisions, preparing visits and telephone calls are made at your desk, not at 3:00 PM on a wet, cold December afternoon when you want to quit for the day. It's essential that you approach the following with an open mind, and then you'll experience the vast difference in overall success my method delivers.

One or two successful visits does not make a salesperson. Overall longevity and percentages are what count. Sales visit records have been around a long time; however as a complete package, my method is unequaled.

There were five distinct processes I'll briefly define before moving into more detail. Check Out List, Visit

List, Steno Book, Master File, Map, and Chart. The brief description that's next is just that, don't be concerned if at first you don't completely understand. You will as we go on.

We'll be using Steno Books for both Check Out and Visit Lists, and though laptops work, too, Steno Books are most appropriate, and you'll see why. At this writing hand-held electronic devices are evolving at a runaway rate. Smart phones with text software may interface with your PC. Laptops led to net-books, which in turn have led to net-tops.

By the time my "Secrets" are revealed, handwritten Steno Book Check Out and Visit Lists could be replaced by these or other devices yet to be introduced. However, hand written Steno Books for their size, simplicity of use, and ease of reference continue to be my choice method for developing active Check Out and Visit Lists.

CHECK OUT LIST: Your written list of companies needing to be telephoned to determine if they buy or have a need for what you sell: a DPB. The list comprises companies you've selected from directories, supplied leads, or other various sources. The Check Out call results in a FI (Forget It) or POVL (Put On Visit List). Your Check Out List will consist of a considerable number of pages.

VISIT LIST: The prepared written list of companies you plan to visit. The list is compiled from companies you've located using the Check Out List, companies from prior Visit Lists, pre-qualified leads or direct inquiries.

STENO BOOK: These books are used to compose the Check Out List and Visit List; they stay whole and become permanent records. During my early years I tore the sheets from these books and stored them in file folders. Now I leave Steno Books intact and mark each book by areas or designated time spans. Depending on territory circumstances, six or so Steno Books can last a long time.

MASTER FILE: This is a computerized list of every company that was entered (written) in the Check Out List, and likewise companies entered onto a Visit List. (Before computers 4X6" filing cards were used for this need).

You will enter all the handwritten names from the Steno Book Check Out and Visit list into a computer list you'll title Master File. Do it after you complete (fill), a page of calls and/or visits in a steno book. Keep the Master File current. You won't start new Check Outs or Visit Lists unless you've entered all existing, completed, Check Outs and Visit Lists into the Master File. (An exception to the previous rule follows later). My computer database alphabetically sorts company names, as they're entered from the written Check Out and Visit List, thereby creating the Master File.

MAP: A map that is marked to correspond to the Visit List being worked. The Map shows a pinpoint geographical location, utilizing a color value rating, for every company to be visited.

Examples of the written Check Out, Visit List, Steno Book, computer Master File, and the Map follow at the end of this chapter. There is also a chart that helps define the system.

Okay, now we'll move into details, and later we'll get involved in the preparation of these five processes. I'll start with the Check Out List.

CHECK OUT LIST

A written list prepared for making Check Out telephone calls. Check Out Lists are always completed for a territory prior to beginning visits. This fact leads us to another of my major rules; NEVER, NEVER MAKE A COLD SALES VISIT WITHOUT A PRIOR Check Out TELEPHONE CALL. Again, there should ALWAYS be a Check Out call before a personal visit. An exception is some type of furnished pre-qualified visit, where the company and person in question is open to a visit at any time. (There's another exception that's explained later).

The Check Out List could be prepared on any type of pad, but Steno Books are by far the best. Steno notebooks are inconspicuous, practically weightless, and fit in a briefcase, a small literature carrier or a small catalog. Steno Books are even usable at the customer's desk, as you wait out an interruption if the customer takes a telephone call. Laptops work, but computer use during a visit in a customer's office suggests that person may be secondary to your other interest. Laptops are old hat and no longer impress, sort of like the cell phone. (Remember when people showed off by talking in public on their cell phones?)

The Check Out List write-ups remain in the Steno Book. Start a new one as needed. Completed Steno Books are easily stored after the company names are entered into a computer (Master File). Not much writing is necessary to record Check Out call results. I write small, so I could fit 10 companies to a page on my Check Out List. Your method for accumulating companies or clients for this list can come from various manufacturers' directories, leads, hearsay, Google searches, and perhaps the Yellow Pages. There will be more about developing your own lists a little further along.

Write in the companies being prepared for Check Out telephone calls by name, telephone number, contact person, address, etc. near the left margin of the pad, going across only a quarter of the page.

With information gathered from manufacturers directories, etc., pinpoint a space just above the company name for the number of employees and circle it. Then, to the right of the company name list the products they manufacture, distribute, and sell. In the same area write any other pertinent information given in the directory or other source. I usually put names of individuals, their titles and phone numbers below the company name. The remaining portion (largest space) is left unused, so that you can write the information you gather from each Check Out telephone call.

Directories for accumulating a list of prospects depends on your field of sales. Harris Publishing and Manufacturers' News Publishing both offer hardcover industrial directories. Harris, a division of Dunn & Bradstreet also sells subscriptions to an on-line database. Manufacturers' News offer their info on CD's. Some cities and states publish their own directories. These types of directories are all broken into sections titled: Geographical, Alphabetical, Product and/or SIC (Standard Industrial Classification). Their CD's offer more alternative search methods. I found the hard cover SIC. section worked best for me. The U.S. Government Office of Management and Budget publish numbers used universally to identify product. One year the SIC identification number 3531 listed manufacturers of Construction Machinery, but these can change with yearly publications. The Yellow Pages served me well when looking for distributors.

The Thomas Register manufacturer's hardcopy directories were many volumes, over three feet wide, and listed manufacturers of every conceivable product. Thomas Register is now ThomasNet and can be found at thomasnet.com. McGraw Hill-Dodge, Builders Exchange, and other similar services are necessary for those selling contractors and architects. McGraw Hill Sweets Network lists manufacturers of building products. Until a few years ago Sweets Directories offered volumes of large books, but discontinued hard copies so now it's on-line too. Check their website at products.construction.com

Computer searches, using Google and other mechanisms will lead you to company websites. I've searched the word "gears," adding specific categories such as machines and/or territories, and found potentials. However, some website facades have maddening long lists of unrelated items, though others are hilarious. Like one site resulting from a Google search for a special category of "gears" that boasted, "married women looking discreetly for dates." Sorry, I don't remember the specifics of that site. If you're now involved in industrial or commercial sales and have not used manufacturers' directories, no wonder you're reading a book on outside sales. I'm glad it's mine for my sake and yours.

Manufacturer's directories usually list the PA, the engineering manager, marketing manager, and others. Sometimes I go to geographic sections, searching city-by-city or county-by-county for companies that manufacture a product that use my widget as part of their product; that's OEM sales. A prime example of an OEM would be Ford Motor Company buying tires from Goodyear, Michelin or General Tire, product (tires) needed to complete their automobiles; parts they themselves don't manufacture.

The above preparation holds true for all ICBBS: industrial, distributor, contractor, service provider, specifier, user, schools, municipalities, retailer, and countless other types. If it's drill bits, most all manufacturers have use for them. If it's pumps, lighting, chemicals, ceiling panels, tools, fasteners, castings, construction equipment, maintenance items, and on and on, you'll be researching contractors, manufacturers, distributors, and users that need or sell them. The product or products you sell dictate how you go about accumulating leads. If you sell a service, whether its administrative, such as computer assistance, or labor intensive like plating, the same procedures apply. If you work for a distributor with lots of products, always use one or two lead items in your Check Outs, something different, like a wrench that beeps when it's lost. Hmmm great idea! When you research directory lists, write any company name that has the possibility of using the widget, widgets or service you sell onto the

Check Out List. Then telephone and hopefully discover a DPB. If your product is something everyone uses, like paint, you still need those key names from Check Outs to garner decision-makers names for a visit. It's that eventual visit that actually defines a DPB, and it's your sales ability that turns DPB's into customers. Don't mull over the list now, things will become clear as we continue. Now let's say you've written the Check Out List for one area (territory) and used 10 pages with 8 companies to a page. Supplied leads with names can be written into the same Check Out List as well, just indicate (write), where each lead originated.

The tough part is next: The telephone calls themselves. Discipline, persistence, product knowledge, and strength are the attributes needed to get this job completed. How effectively you conduct yourself with Check Out calls will determine your degree of sales discovery. Further along we'll detail precisely how the telephone calls are enacted. Lots of firms create leads with telephone blitzes, but in this case only your personal attention makes it work. You may very well, and that's the purpose, get a *key decision-maker* on the phone, and you must be ready to think on your feet; remember, if you confirm a Check Out is a DPB, secure a visit at the same time when possible. If, from the call you surmise there's no potential, mark FI following whatever information gathered from the call. (More on FI later). There were times when I called all day and got nowhere, but it also goes the other way. You can find so much business and you're so anxious to get started visiting, you fail to clearly write the conversation from the telephone call.

I remember once demonstrating how the Check Out system worked to an engineer with a company I represented as a favor to the owner since the engineer was to become their new sales manager. We were so successful locating the decision-makers of companies we phoned, and identifying DPBs, he thought it was a setup; it happens that way.

When you find a possible DPB with the Check Out call, that company is then transferred (written in) immediately onto a Visit List, using a separate Steno Book. Hopefully, from the call you'll have gotten the name of a decision-maker or maybe a name that can help you find the decision-maker. In any case if they have potential as a customer (DPB), they're transferred to the Visit List. (DPB's can become an FI after the first sales visit, when you find the information you obtained during the Check Out call was overstated or plain wrong). The completed Check Out call should include a short note about the conversation, along with names you uncover. When you have a detailed conversation with a Check Out that you transfer to a new Visit List, the highlights and notes are also transferred. I usually don't put more than four companies on a Visit List per steno page allowing room for forthcoming notes from future visits and telephone calls. When I know a particular company (usually a good customer) will require lots of notes, I dedicate a full page to their Visit List entry.

While initially preparing the Check Out list using a directory, I don't want to miss even the slightest potential so I list every feasible company, even if it's unlikely they'll have use for my product. The added value of visiting the websites of potentials, while preparing a Check Out call list, is determined by the product you sell. As mentioned, some items like paint are needed by practically every business, so no need to waste time with website searches, unless you're looking for applications that require a type of special paint. On the other hand, if you're selling a niche item, such as bellows or vibration dampers, a visit to the website could help, especially if they clearly show their product uses the type of widget you sell.

For me, 85% to 90% of the companies on my Check Out List did *not* become a potential customer (DPB). After a negative call I mark FI in large letters next to that company on the Check Out List, along with the short note about my conversation. Even if the result of the call is FI, I still write what they do manufacture, distribute, etc., and move to the next company. So remember, when a company from the Check Out list *does not* have requirements for widgets you're selling and since the information won't be recorded anywhere else, be sure you *list on the Check Out call what they do manufacture.* You never know, by reevaluating old Check Out lists, you may find a potential customer for a new product you acquire years later. Some companies on your Check Out List can become FI because of erroneous information in the directory. The company may be out of business, or you might find distributors incorrectly listed in a Manufacturers' Directory, or other various outdated reasons. I've asked for someone listed in the directory and was told they died five years ago. I hate when that happens! I've switched directory publishers because of out-of-date information.

When *I do find* a potential DPB through a Check Out telephone call, I prominently write POVL and other telephone call details next to that company on the Check Out List. Then I transfer (rewrite) that company name, address, contact names, etc., and similar details about that phone call onto the new sales Visit List that's being developed in preparation for visiting. I repeat: Use limited space for the notes carried over from the Check Out call onto the Visit List, leaving plenty of room to write in the results from upcoming visits. Once a company (business) listed on the Check Out List has been phoned and defined as either a FI or POVL, no further attention is given to that company on the Check Out List.

You've learned that the Check Out (telephone calls) creates the Visit List; therefore that process eliminates any possibility of making cold-call visits. Though it's not the norm, you can get a contact name from a website. If a directory lists a sales or service person, telephone and ask them who makes decisions for your product. (We get into the actual calls in a moment).

Here's the exception to which I alluded earlier. An unannounced visit can be prudent. Creative selling comes to bear, but *only* when you have a person's name from a prior Check Out or contact. Much like the 4:45 unannounced visit in the rain I described. I've made unannounced visits to companies, knowing the buyer is on vacation, providing me the opportunity to ask for someone else who can verify or rebuke the PA's sentiments about my widget. Remember my gear sample in Chapter Two? The PA had asked an unknowing agent to quote on a gear being discontinued, don't let that happen to you. Checking with an engineer, foreman or, if warranted, a different buyer, etc., can be a lifesaver. It could have saved that agent *weeks, maybe months*—no exaggeration—of work and frustration.

Now, we'll cover making the Check Out phone call itself, and it can be a tough business. I remember times doing Check Out calls in large cities all day from my hotel room. Today's cell phone contracts make local and distant telephone calls equal in cost. However, doing Check Out's while visiting large cities provides the advantage of an immediate visit, when you hit a hot DPB while in town. While in a city for a week or more, I did Check Out calls first, adding any new potential DPB to my already prepared Visit List (more about existing Visit Lists next). Sometimes, the new addition to the existing Visit List could be just across the street from another company I planned to see. If your selling territory is local, it's less complex. Check Out calls to companies scattered across miles of rural areas should be completed before heading to that territory. Cutting down on driving time is a major player in the success formula. Remember the percentage factor and the importance of making as many effective sales visits a day as possible. Don't scoff at the percentage significance.

I remember sometimes starting near the bottom of the Check Out List, and doing a couple of calls so the list didn't seem so long. I tried to complete one page before starting the second, however it usually didn't work out that way, as some people I needed were unavailable. Often companies that sounded the best in a directory turned out to be FI and others that scarcely made it as a POVL were promising surprises.

I was a pioneer in the Check Out call process. Early in my career there was little, if any, set protocol from company operators. Most operators were helpful, but the deluge of today's phone marketers has changed things. Computer software has evolved to a point that's scary. Once your personal phone or address are on a list, the U.S. mail and telephone become your enemies. Personal data are gathered; when you use your credit card, rent a movie, or use reward-cards. Methods for accumulating data on individuals grow daily, and material stolen by hackers is a threatening problem. As ICBBS salespeople were phoning companies not individuals, so Check Out telephone calls are less tedious. Companies expect solicitation, some even encourage it.

Depending on various contracts that cell phones companies offer, a day's worth of cell phone Check Out calls could cost you a lot of minutes. If you travel, use your hotel room phone if local calls are free, but not if it takes an hour to reach your hotel near the end of a day. Sometimes telephoning a very large company requires working your way from one person to another. Looking for their decision-maker can take an hour or more. For those of us who preceded cell phones, making Check Out calls in freezing temperatures standing on the rock-hard frozen concrete surface of a telephone booth, with wind swirling through the open part at the bottom, is history we'll all thankfully forget. I became proficient at the telephone booth shuffle. How about frozen ink? It happens.

Your telephone pursuit depends on what you sell. My experience in electric motors and gears sometimes dictated that I get to someone other than purchasing, as do other products, especially if your widget is specified prior to the requisition being sent to a buyer. Sales, marketing, or maybe the parts manager make decisions regarding the use of your widget. In architectural or construction sales you must get to the correct specifier or project manager. A general contractor may shop for a "substitute," but four times out of five the building product purchased will be the one specified. If your selling major investment machinery or equipment, the owner or CEO (Chief Executive Officer), will be involved. If you're selling computer assistance or website design, the size of the company you're contacting will determine the decision-maker. The PA will sometimes be the decision-maker of services, but you'll need to be sure. If you're selling heat treat service, a plant manager's approval is possible.

It was often unclear where the decisions were made, but in some cases you could quote all day, but without some hidden decision-maker's approval, purchasing would not make a change, even with a price advantage. You will find that smaller firms purchasing and engineering work together or are even the same person. With electric motor OEM sales the owner of a small or medium-sized company could be the decision-maker.

This next suggestion helps get past telephone operators. The manufacturers' directories usually list contact names, but when the individual's job description isn't your target use the name anyway. QUESTION the person you reach. To avoid being interrupted during their daily routine, most people will quickly pass you to someone else, possibly the person you need.

Telephoning to find the decision-makers from your own prepared Check Out List is a **separation point**: where the diligent salesperson succeeds and the slacker fails. It's easier, when you have a lead generated by your company's magazine ad, their website or other marketing efforts. Those types of Check Out calls most often lead to names of decisions makers. Don't waste the lead if it's a wrong name, question the person. Find out if their company buys your product, then get other names. Be direct. Ask who they believe makes the decisions about your products, NOT WHO PLACES THE ORDER. Always ask for other names. If maintenance is important, get those names. If you go through proper channels, the accepted method, you'll likely be sidetracked back to the beginning. Use leads, go from name to name, then when you're ready to make your pitch, you can legitimately say you've been talking to so-and-so and they gave me your name and suggested you may be interested in... I was always amazed at the lack of persistence when reading an outside salespersons written report that merely indicated a lead had misunderstood the ad and wasn't interested in our widgets. What a waste. Get names! Get information! Get off the main road!

In the past one never knew how a buyer, or whoever it was you telephoned, would reply. If you caught someone under pressure or moody, rude responses were possible. However, there were always those who make the effort to be amiable regardless of their circumstances, and they're appreciated.

Today's different. Today everyone answers your call with a courteous and cheerful greeting. You're skeptical? Well, can you recall a curt recorded greeting? "Hello, this is Millie Flowerblossom (or perhaps Frederick Marvelous), I'm sorry, but I'm unable to take your call. Please leave a message at the tone. I told you, everyone is at their best on their voice mail message. Some folks never answer their phone or return calls I mean never! That's their policy.

Here are 10 possibilities to exploit recorded messages:

1. Keep trying repeatedly to catch someone in. Thursday and Friday are best. If you know their phone records the calling phone number, disconnect after the third ring. Some phone systems ring your phone back when you disconnect before the message ends, and digitally store your phone number. When I hung up on the same person more than once, a few curious people called me asking why I'd phoned and sometimes with good results. However they could be agitated, so be ready. Something like, "I didn't leave a message not knowing if you were the correct person to contact," or "I didn't want to be misunderstood, so I disconnected, and planned to try later."

2. Place calls in early morning, just before or just after lunch, and near the end of the day. People are more likely to pick up since personal calls are made and received just before and after lunch, and near the end of their day.

3. When you know someone never answers the phone, have them paged; however, if it's done too often you'll get someone upset. Some companies discourage paging. Alternately, tell the operator, "I've tried several times today, but so-and-so is always on voice mail." Then ask without pausing, "I'm wondering, is so-and-so in today?" For some reason, with that *particular question*, once the operators confirm they're in, some make an effort to get them on the phone.

4. Ask the operator to ring another phone in the area. Suggest they try a secretary or cohort in the next office. Unless it's a large company, operators know everyone's physical location. Talk to whoever answers the phone and be honest about your purpose. Ask them if they see, or know the whereabouts of the person you're seeking. They'll likely flag them down for you.

On occasion the person I reached was very helpful, and in a few cases was the decision-maker. Yet be ready; this particular method can also irritate.

5. Tell the operator that Walter Waterfountain keeps answering on his voice mail and ask for a name with the same job description in his department. Getting new contact names is the backbone of outside sales success. I've had lots of success finding *key people* asking the operator for someone who works with the person I've tried to reach. You may get another voice mail, but you get an additional key name. I've asked for their boss, too, a legitimate request that operators may not question, but different operators equal different responses. Remember Mrs. Ghoul?

6. If you need to reach two people at the same company, ask the initial contact if they know the whereabouts of the second person. Be direct and continue with, "Would you mind asking her/him if she/he can take my call?" I'm afraid if I go through the operator, I'll get a voice mail." Devise your own version, depending on what you know about the demeanor of the individual you're calling.

7. When you reach an operator or secretary who asks,"Who's calling," *be prepared* to add a short, concise message that will tempt Ms. Flowerblossom to take your call. Ask the operator to pass it on, along with your name. If you know the product you're selling might influence Mrs. Flowerblossom, add it to the message. Asking the operator or secretary a question that *requires* an answer from your target may bring that person to the phone. Do it something like this: "Please tell her I'll be visiting your plant around 2:00 PM on Tuesday and need to check our recent quote." Even if that fails, at the least there's some chance you'll get a call back to avoid your visit.

8. If the person you wish to reach is someone with whom you haven't spoken previously, record a message that *you've been told* they are the decision-maker

concerning your widget. It works two ways: First, if your information is inaccurate, people have a tendency to correct others and they may return the call to tell you so, yet give you a name. Second, if you've called the right person, that fact suggests someone passed their name on to you, possibly their boss. That possibility increases the likelihood of a callback.

9. Here's a good one. Try sales, or the sales manager, especially if you have their name. Sales people answer the phones much more often and are sometimes willing to help with names. They may appreciate your approach, even try it themselves. Then use the sales person's name as a reference when you place the next call and get voice mail. There's a good chance you'll receive a return call, because people feel obliged to their peers. If your subject answers, so much the better.

10. Calling the CEO at a large company of a 1000 employees, or more will usually get you their personal secretary. They field very few inquiries and will usually return the call or often answer their phone. When you have that opportunity, it's an important time to be yourself. Explain who you are and what you want. Do it honestly and with class. **Nothing Canned!** If you quickly develop an adult exchange, a personal secretary is likely to be forthcoming with names of people who work for their boss.

I didn't give this next option a number, because it's dangerous and should only be tried as a last resort. If the person you're calling won't respond after varied attempts, and I mean over a long period of time, use the voice mail and be upfront about your exaspera-tion. State the reason you're leaving the message, then add, "If you're not returning my calls because of a past problem with my company, I'd like an opportunity to clarify things." You can obviously create trouble, but it may get their attention, and after all, getting someone's attention is what we're doing.

Here's a bonus method that may draw criticism, but what the heck, try it, if need be. In cases where a company doesn't offer an operator option and the phone system is so complex, it precludes reaching a live person, then use dial by name and press in the name Smith. Talk to whomever you reach. Again, be honest, tell them why you did it.

Unfortunately, difficulty in reaching business people seems to be a trend, leaving the impression today's workers avoid responsibility, opinions, comments, or any involvement beyond their job description. Remember Horatio and Clementine? They didn't have human instincts or emotions, limiting their potential. American workers forged ahead of world competition by being quick-thinking, aggressive, risk-taking individuals. It's our heritage to do so, and I sure hope as a nation we don't forsake it.

Now we'll apply some of the above methods to the real world of Check Out calls. The phone rings, and either a receptionist or phone system answers. If you have a name from a directory or other publication, ask for that person. If you're fortunate, and a person answers rather than their voice mail, be direct and quick. I often said the following, but don't try to memorize it. Write your own version, try it on the next call, and build from there. You'll begin to realize that being yourself improves your approach with each call.

"My company manufactures widgets. You're listed in the BLANK directory as a manufacturer of WHATEVER, and I've taken your name from that entry. It seems apparent your company would use widgets." Keep going, don't pause yet. "If that's correct, would you be the person interested in knowing how my new widget is different, how it changes or improves thing? Are you the PERSON whom I should make aware of it? That, madam/sir (madam or sir fits here), is the reason for my call."

Your widgets will determine your phone presentation. Write your thoughts after each conversation exchange, giving rise to a evolving approach. If they ask about your product, be prepared to be factual and very concise. If you think you've got the correct person but they push you off to purchasing, be direct again. "Thanks for the name. I recognize purchasing would be placing orders, but does the PA, specify widgets without approval from you, or someone else?" (Obviously if you've called a company with 20 employees, the PA is likely the correct person or willing to tell you who is.)

Here again some individuals can become annoyed, but you'll be pleasantly surprised how often the honest approach works. As a conversation develops get as many names as possible. If you're going to maintenance, get a name of a decision-maker there. Having a chance to talk to that bunch can take some doing, but with a name you can begin the process of getting an appointment. Obviously once you find a company with potential for sales—a DPB—continue your efforts until you have an audience. I've had my first phone call tell me to come in. *Remember Rule 2 for hard-to-reach individuals, phone early A.M. or just before, and after noon or late afternoon.* It's the best time to catch them by their phone with their voice mail system off.

Very early on, as an manufacturers' agent, when the future of my sales company hung by a string, I pursued what I called a leverage for Check Out Calls. If I was certain my product was best-suited for a particular DPB, only then did I convinced myself, leverage was permissible, since in actuality it helped everyone. Remember as a kid how innovative your parents could be, conning you into eating your vegetables? Now I like vegetables.

Here's how it went. If my target contact was engineering, I asked for a specific engineer listed in a directory, the chief engineer, or perhaps just the engineering department depending on the size of the company. Once connected, I indicated the company I represent had once been in contact with this department about a project. There was no record of the source or specifics of names and dates, only hearsay, but I didn't want an inquiry to slip through the cracks.

Very often, I was guided to the most likely engineer that works with widgets. They might say, "It's not me, but Garth is involved with those type of widgets right now. I'll connect you."

Once, with a small company my leverage approach backfired, and a guy growled at me, "I'm the only one who can make gear design changes and I don't remember ever talking to your company." I mumbled an apology, but it didn't help. I decided the direct Check Out calls procedure I've outlined worked best. Besides, misleading people felt bad and took the fun out of Check Outs. Enough of true confessions!

Again, if you work for a distributor and sell many different products, my formula still applies. To get an appointment, distributor salespeople should select a lead item. Selling a service changes nothing, you must still get to the decision-maker. If you have something to offer with new technology present it. For those who sell products that deal only with purchasing, just do it, as they say. Assume the buyer has their company at heart. Ask for a face-to-face meeting and see where it takes you. If they're completely negative, yet you know they buy widgets of the type you sell, and yours is better, try the same buyer another time. Moods change. After two or three tries go to a different buyer, their boss or supervisor. Get a reasonable answer why your widget is not acceptable. With a logical response from the decision-maker you can begin the process of changing their minds. Don't over-push if your competitors product is obviously the best choice. Needs change, and vendors screw up, giving you a new opportunity. Purchasing people change, too, and loyalties to a competitor are forgotten. Just be sure you're talking to the decision-maker. After months of no contact I re-contacted buyers just to see if they had left the company. You'll do much better than your competitor that overlooks this detail.

Sometimes when contacting small companies of 20 or less employees, the buyer who selects your widgets could also be the owner. These companies are nice to deal with, as everyone's familiar with the goings-on, and finding the decision-maker is easy. Companies of 30 to 50 people likely have two decision-makers, both familiar with, and interested in, knowing about widgets that can improve their production, or just save them money. It's advisable to mix in some of these smaller companies with larger ones, while doing Check Out calls, it makes continual telephone calling easier. The product you sell dictates the approach. For me, electric motor OEM decisions might be made by a sales manager, not usually true when I sell open gear OEM's; those are engineering and purchasing types.

A gear story: After what I thought was a good DPB, I pursued a buyer for years trying for his gear business. Countless visits and innovative quotes were involved. We even suggested design improvements for their gears that they later incorporated with my competition. Now that's frustrating! He was a proficient buyer, and finally admitted that the owner had picked the present gear source. The owner wouldn't take my calls, and strangely did not have voice mail. Finally, I gave his secretary a specific message, suggesting that as a gear manufacturer, I had new information on tooth grinding procedures. He took my call, but was abrupt once he determined he already utilized what I considered new. He referred me back to purchasing. A few weeks later I called the buyer and told him I'd had a conversation with his owner; that helped. The buyer assumed I'd learned more about their company, and that led him to the fact the owner was born in Germany, (I'd realized he was German from his accent), and every year he visited the German gear manufacturer once or twice, making his overseas trip a business expense.

"So, the buyer added, he is very unlikely to change gear vendors."

This stuff happens, but why a purchasing agent doesn't present the truth in the beginning is sometimes a mystery. What a waste! My visits and phone calls to the PA were useless. That company was eventually bought by a competing manufacturer with their own gear capability. All gear requirements were brought in-house. Had I gotten the business earlier, I would have lost it later; that happens, too.

Obviously a lot of time goes down the tubes in these instances, but it's all necessary maneuvering. Managers, encourage your outside salespeople to pursue DPBs without wavering. *Now is the time for action. The future can't change the present; it depends on it.* Remember, always check back with a negative DPB. Unexpected changes do occur, and 6 months is too long.

Before you decide outside sales sounds too tough for you, I'll offer this encouragement. I've had a rewarding career, full of business excitement and sales highs that beat most sport's thrills. There's also travel, and more money that would have been possible behind a desk. As a thriving salesperson your company wouldn't want to lose you to a competitor, and up the ladder you go.

After you complete the telephone calls from your written list of Check Out calls, you have hopefully generated a number of companies marked POVL. That leads into the Visit List.

VISIT LIST

A new Visit List consists of companies transferred from Check Out call lists that you decided were POVL. They are added to companies being revisited from a previous Visit List. Additionally, companies that had made direct inquiries (always a welcome occurrence) are more additions to a new Visit List. Whatever the reason for preparing a new Visit List, don't crowd more than four companies onto a single page, using the Steno Book. Assuming your Visit Lists are several pages, the top page should be dated when you make the first visit write-up. Number the pages too. The company name and address should include a telephone number at the left margin, with direct dial numbers under individual names. Indicate the number of employees over the company name. Include a brief note of what they manufacture, distribute, or use.

The most important part of these lists are the notes you add from the Check Out List, from a previous visit, or intermediate telephone calls. Notes like, "She expressed having difficulty getting calls returned from one of our competitors," can be an important remark your creative juices can use on your next visit. Don't comment on the problem, but describe your company's new phone system that keeps beeping until you complete the contact or your own personal system that NEVER allows you to forget return calls. She's likely forgotten she mentioned the competitor's problem to you and may not comment, but will mentally note your information. That's finessing. A chapter about finessing follows.

All these preparations, writing up Check Out calls and preparing Visit Lists, are done at your desk, but as each visit is actually made, the important aspects of that meeting should be recorded in the Visit List *immediately after the visit, along with the date of the visit.* Perhaps you could remember long enough to write or record them in your car or in the lobby of the next visit, while waiting for your next audience. I've gotten a little ahead of myself, so, more about the Visit List itself.

After a new Visit List is completed a rating according to DPB importance should be assigned to each company. I use R (red) as most important and put a R just over the company name. I followed with G (green) for second most important, with the least of importance being B (black or blue). Visit List records, like the Check Out

records are entered onto the Master File too. (See Visit List examples at the end of this chapter).
MAP

We need to interrupt Visit Lists momentarily, and introduce the Map, because it fits in well at this point. The following will save you lots of valuable time when it costs the most; while you're on the street, devising your own secrets. The Visit List should be used in conjunction with a city Map, or perhaps a state Map when your potential customers are spread out across a state. I needed both. The city and county Maps for working metro areas, and state Maps when making longer trips into small cities where customers and potentials are separated by many miles not blocks. Maps for places like St. Louis are large. While in my car I had to spread the map out across my lap for a good overview. That action caused the only rear-end collision I've had. Downtown St. Louis produces distracting sidewalk sites on hot summer days. The UPS driver I rear-ended admitted to the same diversion.

If you have, say, 100 potentials on your Visit List, use a full city metropolitan Map. If they are fewer than 50 or so, photocopy the condensed side of the metropolitan Map, it's usually on the flip side. It generally encompasses the same area but condensed to 10 or 20% of the size of the main Map. If your area's one portion of a large city, use the large city Map, making copies of your area only. I found it was best when using the smaller, condensed Map, to refer to the full size for street details.

Here's how it works. On the Map you choose, as small as possible, write the company name of every prospective company you plan to visit at its street location. That's correct! Every company listed on your Visit List goes on the Map. If it's 100 or more the Map is even more important. It can be a slow and tedious job, but just do it. (Companies like the Holiday Inn offer similar maps for hotel locations on their websites.) To coordinate the Map rating with the Visit List, circle each with a colored pen: red, green or blue. Then, as small as possible next to the circle, write a page number that corresponds to the visit list page where that company is written. If you have a hundred with four to a page you can see why noting the page number is essential. That's 25 pages of companies to contact. Color coding is most accurate while sitting at your desk with time to contemplate the importance of each customer potential.

See what this does for you! Let's say it's 3:00 PM, and you just left a visit. Looking at the Map you recognize there are four green rated companies in another section of the city. With not enough time to see them all, it would be best to get them together another day. Closer by, you see two greens and a black. Check your notes to determine if a phone call ahead is necessary before a visit. Some people insist you call ahead. Read your previous comments on the Visit List, making sure the person you want to see doesn't discourage late-afternoon visits. Then go for the greens then the black. I'll remind you: Don't rush off to see someone with whom you like to shoot the breeze; that's WFS. If there's time, hit a close-by red, even though you recognize you're entering uncharted waters and seeing an engineer or purchasing person whom you've only spoken with on the phone, and who you recognize as a difficult sort. *With the close-by red only a few blocks away staring you in the face, you're less likely to talk yourself out of that late-afternoon visit.* If all your DPBs require appointments a day or more ahead, the Map helps set up those calls. A small check mark is put on the Map over companies that insist you call ahead, sometimes five minutes ahead will do. Don't drop in on them even when they're established customers.

Looking at the finished Map spread out before you with companies circled in three colors, gives an immediate image of an attack plan. Sometimes using the smaller, condensed Map, I abbreviated the company names. Then, rather than circle them in color, I inked color dots next to a plain circle. In that way I could white out the colors or company names, thereby utilizing the same Map for the next Visit List and several thereafter. If I wasn't going to use the same map again, I checked names off the Map as I concluded business. That's a great way to see how you're progressing. To use the same Map, I tried using small stickers, rather than check marks but they weren't always dependable. There are lots of variations. Your own feel for the potential customer and creative impulses will help you adjust the system once it's up and running.

As I've said, when working with a condensed Map, I still use the large Map to find my way through streets that do not appear on the condensed Map. To repeat: Seeing company names, coded by color importance helps to develop your visit strategy, especially, as often happens, some are clumped together. The Map made companies out in the boonies, where driving time becomes part of the big picture more noticeable. Are computers ready for my Map needs? Map Quest and other guidance systems, assist when you have an address (destination), but I'm not aware of anything with the overall size and planning potential the hardcopy Map offers. Besides, once again, your computer may not be available in some situations, and a map tucks into your coat pocket. Yeah, I still wear a coat and tie on sales visits.

My map also answers the question, "Who do I need to call to set appointments for the area I'll enter today?" Remember I always put a check mark over the company on the Map as a reminder that they insist on being called for an appointment or any other peculiarity required before visiting. If it's an "always" thing, I put a check above the company name on the Visit List, too. Once you're familiar with a DPB and know the pertinent people, you'll know whenever it's best to make unannounced visits. Where are all the reds? Plan a day that will cover reds clumped in different groups. Remember, don't cross the city at 3:00 P.M., get a close-by green or blue/black. This system works for state Maps, too, but the miles of separation will require imagination in your ratings, but still use the Maps, and colors for an overview.

Now, back to the VISIT LISTS: If like me, you cross into several different areas or states that you've divided into sections, affix tab (stickers) to each Visit List page that identifies or begins a separate area. (A Steno Book of Ohio visits are tabbed into sections and/or cities.) You'll have effectively created a tabbed catalog divided into territories. It also works when separating sections within a city. Sticker dividers makes working with the Steno Book much easier.

All the notes you make after each visit remain in the Visit List Steno pad until it's complete. Completing a Visit List may simply mean you're out of space to write notes on the most frequently visited accounts, or as I did when traveling many states, make a new list each time you return to a major city (that could be months). Sometimes, to keep using the same pad, I'd flip the page and add more notes on the backside. That's needed, when one company on a page requires more notes than the others, and you don't want to start a new list (pad). For those who confine themselves to defined parts of a state, a single city or sections of a city, a new Visit List could be based on a time element, say three to six months, or even a year or more. It's possible some businesses on your list were not contacted, and now it's time to prepare a new one. Those companies were most likely coded blue. Add companies you missed into the new list. Remember, for visits, I had two lists, one for the rural state and one for the large city. I wrote both in the same Steno Book, with tabs to separate them into sections. I gave them different names, e.g., Southeast corner Ohio, Columbus Ohio area, etc.

Again, the next Visit List you prepare usually contains the following: New POVL from a Check Out List, companies you missed from a previous Visit List, and naturally, DPBs visited on the previous Visit List that need continued effort. Additionally, supplied leads you've called, and verified need a visit are also added to a new Visit List. Companies you decide not to visit for a while can be dropped from a new Visit List. For that reason I always carefully read over a number of the older Visit lists when preparing a new one, that keeps you from overlooking a company you had put on hold six months or more ago.

A needed pre-Master File comment: When retiring a Steno Book Visit list, be sure all the names have been entered and updated into the computer Master File. If from a previous Check Out you've entered a company as a POVL into the Master File, then, following the visit you determine that company is no longer of interest, add an FI with the date to that company in the Master File entry. Don't delete the POVL just add the dated FI; they tell the story. Again, see the examples at the end of this chapter.

There were times when visiting a city I'd just telephone blue color-coded businesses listed on my Visit List rather than leave town without contacting them. The comments from the phone call would be dated, then headed "called", but written in the same space as notes written from a visit. Other important phone conversations can be recorded and dated on the Visit List as they occur between visits. It's there to see when you prepare the next Visit List. Keep your writing small to handle many comments on one company entry.

Future computer electronic innovations are the only portion of this book I must leave to changing times and individual computer know-how. However, evolving computers will continue to be compatible with my system. Now, the Master File.

MASTER FILE

Lists of companies that are entered into a computer database gathered from the Check Out and Visit List. The lists makes it possible to easily determine if you've ever contacted a company before, what occurred, and where to find the written details.

To build a Master File, you identity (mark) each Steno Book. Use a bold marking pen on the hard cover face of the Steno Book. I identify a Check Out Steno Book by year. Then use tabs to divide into time spans. You could make 300 Check Out Calls in 2007, and if that required 30 pages, you'd write each page number in the upper right-hand corner of that specific tabbed year. Mark each page 1 through 30 as you progress, then you can tab the 31st page 2008. Again, you repeat page numbering for 2008, starting with page 1, until the year 2008 is concluded. Another tab, and you start 2009. I marked my most recent Check Out Steno Book 2007+, since I had retired the previous Check Out book marked 2000, through 2006.

Searching for Star Mfg., a scrolled search in the Check Out Master File may appear as follows.

Star Mfg., 2009, page 4, FI.

Go to the Steno Book marked 2007+, the tabbed year 2009, page 4, and there read why it became a FI.

For Visit Lists I preferred to mark the face of the Steno Book by area, such as Ohio, Indiana, etc., then add tabs to divide into subcategories like North East section, and/or by cities. I also record the date of the visit in the Master File. It's important that each new Steno Book Visit List also carries dates so you can easily choose an older, retired Steno Book. Scrolling for Star Mfg. Co. in the Visit List Master File, the company's entry may appear as follows:

Star Mfg., Cincinnati – page 4., 6/5/07, Open, 8/9/09 FI

In this case Star Mfg. was originally considered a DPB from the Check Out List, and therefore put on a

Visit List. But after several visits they were determined to be an FI, and a date is added for an FI. Here again, I used the tab to quickly turn to any city or section. I made my own tabs and taped them to pages moving progressively downward like an alphabetical memo pad. Periodic updates of Master File Lists must be made to achieve the history given above. Had the Visit List Steno Book entry been marked with dates preceding 2007, I could have gone to a previous year's Steno Book that included the proper page, date, retired or not, to find why it was an FI.

Normally "Open" occurs on the Visit List Master File, as DPBs or customers are continuously pursued. A visit from a lead giving an individual's name who is available at any time without calling ahead can also create a singular "Open" classification without a previous POVL.

If you forget to update a POVL after visits, it can result in a long-standing POVL in the Master File, where an Open classification would have been better. An "Open" from a Check Out indicates that you've been unable to reach a conclusion after numerous Check Out calls, and want the company name listed in the Master File, but you've moved on to another Check Out list.

Remember, when you enter a Check Out call or Visit into the Master File, database software sorts entries alphabetically, creating the Master File. Now any company I've called or visited can be easily found by scrolling the Master File. If more than one individual makes notes into a Check Out, or Visit List use the same Master File, just add a name or initials. Check the chart provided after this chapter. (Four)

Another option: Mix the Check Out and Visit List in the same data base Master File, being sure to indicate (as shown in the examples) in which Steno Book the entry resides (co or vl). If you combine it's also necessary that the Visit List Master File entry include a territory. In my case, IN for Indiana, Indpls for section (city), and date of the visit. You may prefer separating Check Outs from Visit Lists for simplicity, but then it takes a few extra moments to scroll both Master File lists to check on a new company name you encounter.

Remember, as you update the Master File, you can add and delete dates as needed to each listing (dates of contact). Maybe just two entries, the oldest and latest would suit you. Thereafter, when you begin developing a new Check Out List, and you come across Star Mfg. in a directory, scroll both the Check Out and Visit List Master File data base. In the Check Out Master File you could find Star Mfg. 2009, page 4 with an FI, so no need to call again. Visit Lists must be scrolled, too, since it's possible a company can be entered into the Visit List without having ever being entered as a Check Out. A company could call you with details of their needs, so you visit them (man, that's nice when it happens). However, like I said, if you combine the Check Out and Visit list, a company entry could show up in the Master File with an added co from a Check Out, or vl for a visit, or both.

See, it's obvious, without the data base Master File computer record, locating a company would require long hand searches through numerous Check Out and Visit List in all your Steno Books, new and old. Questions like, "What did I say to that buyer the last time I was there, and when was that?" or, "I think I remember that company across the street," are quickly resolved. Most importantly, you can't prepare a new Check Out List unless you know if/when you've contacted a company previously.

Hopefully repeating some points hasn't distracted your concentration, but rather improved comprehension.

A few notable points before closing Boot Camp. Telephone calls substituted for sales visits won't work, it's a phenomena that some salespeople resist accepting. Maybe it's a lack of persistence, determination, available time, or just plain laziness. If one salesperson telephones a prospective buyer ten times to pitch the product, and another of equal talent makes one face-to-face presentation, the visitor has a marked advantage. This shouldn't be news to anyone in the business, it's just that human factor I refer to throughout. The telephone Check Out call must come before new visits, but beyond that it's the visit that generates sales. Well-timed or strategic visits to customers and DPB's develops confidence and build business relationships. With all things equal it's the sales visit that's remembered. Naturally if you've established a rapport with an ongoing customer, phone calls may suffice to fill gaps in time, or in certain situations be preferable. The individual you're contacting will dictate your decision.

Again, I remind you, don't try the canned stuff on calls or visits. You'll be tagged as an amateur, someone that uses prepared answers from a sales book. It's great to work on your diction and pronunciation, an area where books help, but be yourself, answer questions freely with what comes to mind. You obviously want to get it right, or you wouldn't be reading this book.

Finish the book, then come back and attack this chapter again. Prepare your own Check Out or Visit List, as you reread it. If you're aspiring to a particular job, mark these pages and come back to it when you land the sales job you're seeking.

Written Visit Lists should be legible if others have cause to read your write-ups. Mine were for my personal use; hence, my writing was normally very difficult to decipher. Be *very careful* with e-mail. Someone can accidentally click your message or information to the wrong person. I learned the hard way.

"A bit paranoid," one might say about the last paragraph. "Better safe than sorry," I'd answer. Besides, *I maintain there's a fine line between intuitiveness and paranoia.*

EXAMPLES

CHECK OUTS, VISIT LISTS, MASTER FILES, MAP, AND CHART

Page 83: A completed Check Out telephone call list with three POVL's transferred to a Visit List.

Page 84: A Visit List consisting of three companies from a Check Out list and one direct inquiry. Ratings given prior to contact were R, G, B, and R. One entry has yet to be contacted.

Page 85: An incomplete Check Out call list. Two companies were transferred to a Visit List and two still need contact.

Page 86: A Visit List consisting of two companies from a Check Out List, one direct inquiry, and one transferred from a previous Visit List. Ratings given prior to visits were three R's, and one G. Three have yet to be visited and one needs follow-up.

Page 87: A Check Out Master File alphabetical page from a Steno Book divided by years, beginning with the year 2005.

Page 88: A Visit List Master File alphabetical page from a Steno Book divided by territory (e.g., Ohio), then tabbed by cities and sections of state. Example; Cinn = Cincinnati, NC = North Central

Page 89: A combination Check Out and Visit List Master File from a Steno Book marked by years and territory, where co = Check Out, and vl = Visit List, with all their other necessary designations.

Page 90-91: A Visit List on a condensed Map. Companies on the map are marked with reference to a page in a Visit List. R, G, B, (Red, Green, and Black) are used in place of color coding.

Page 92: Chart.

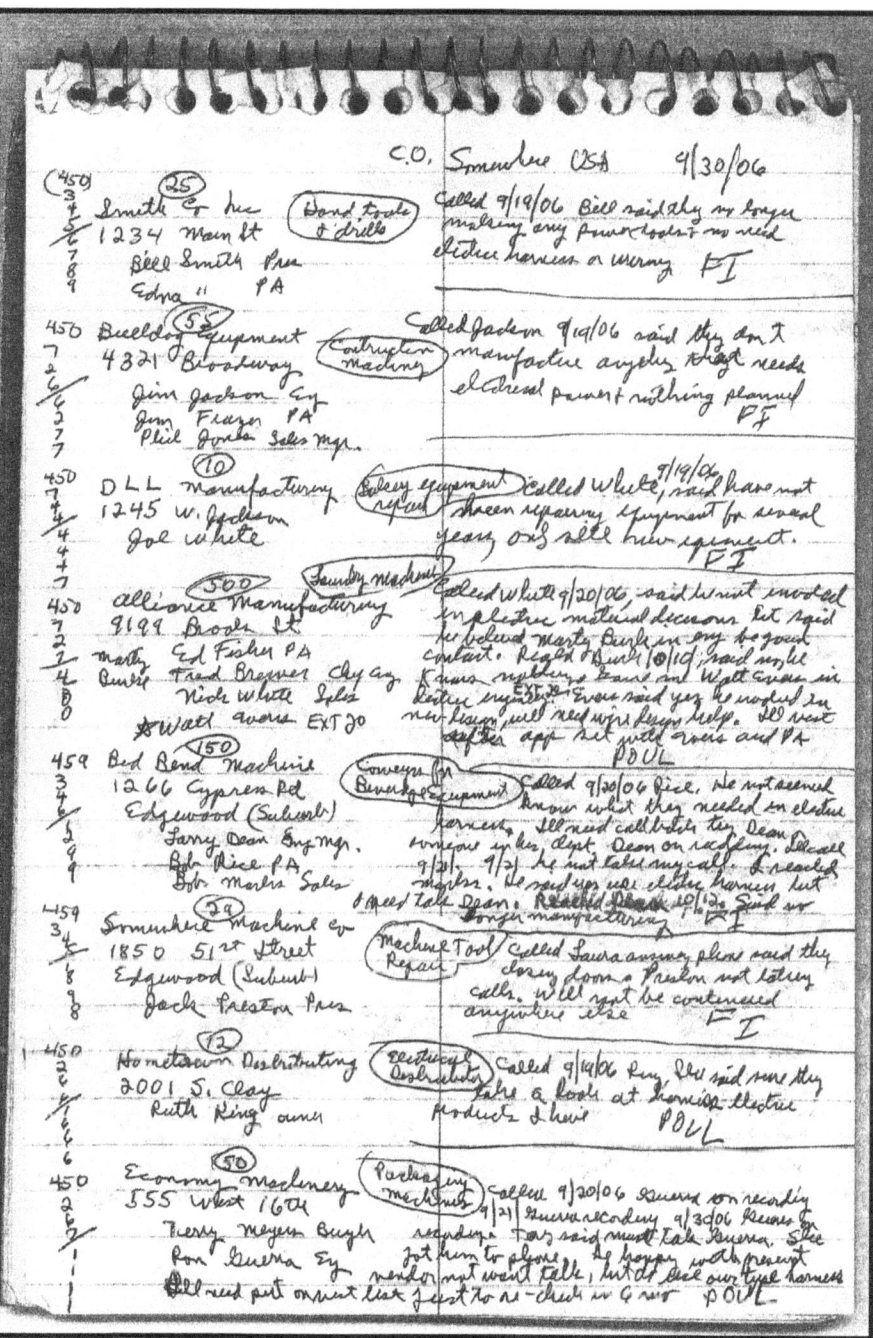

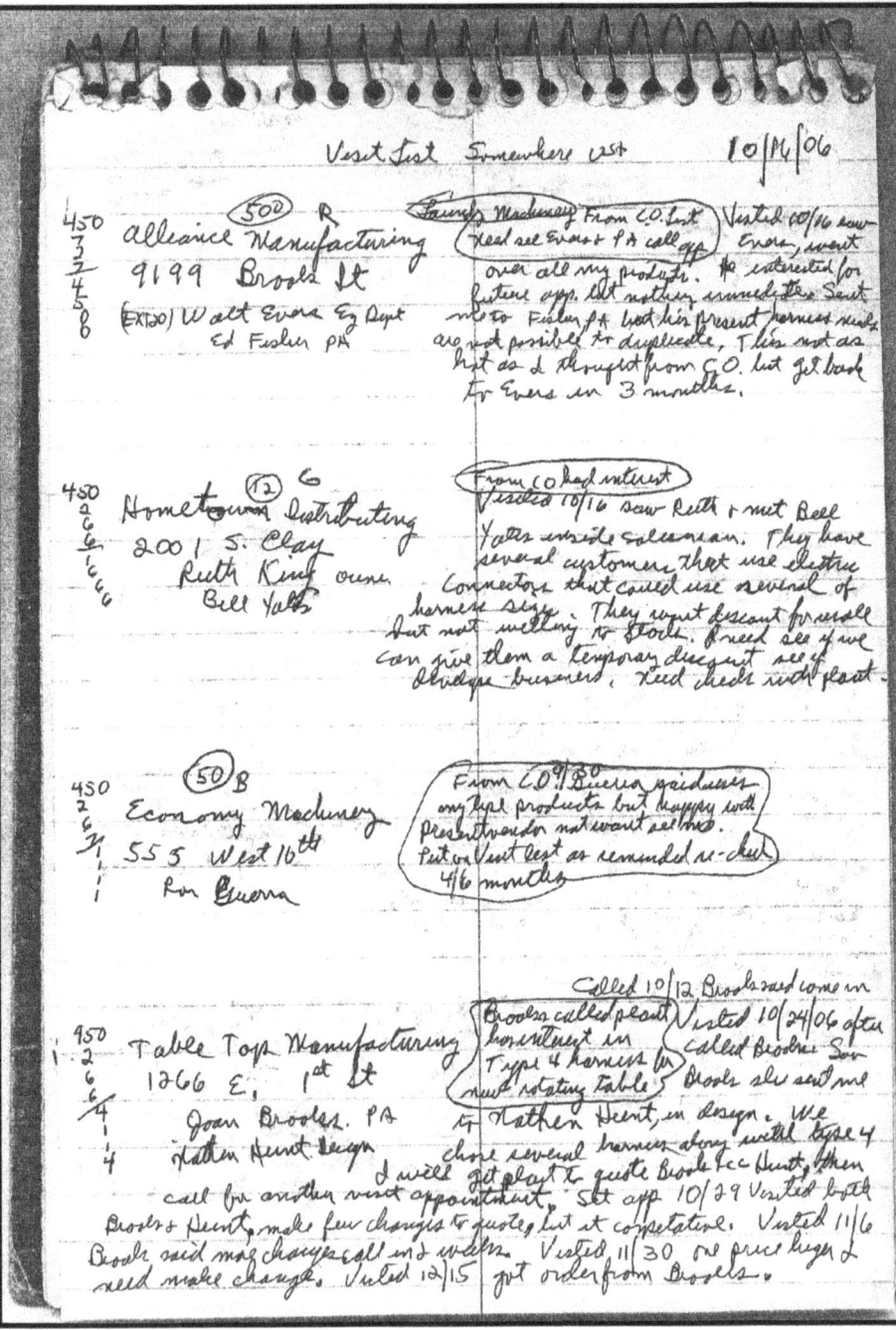

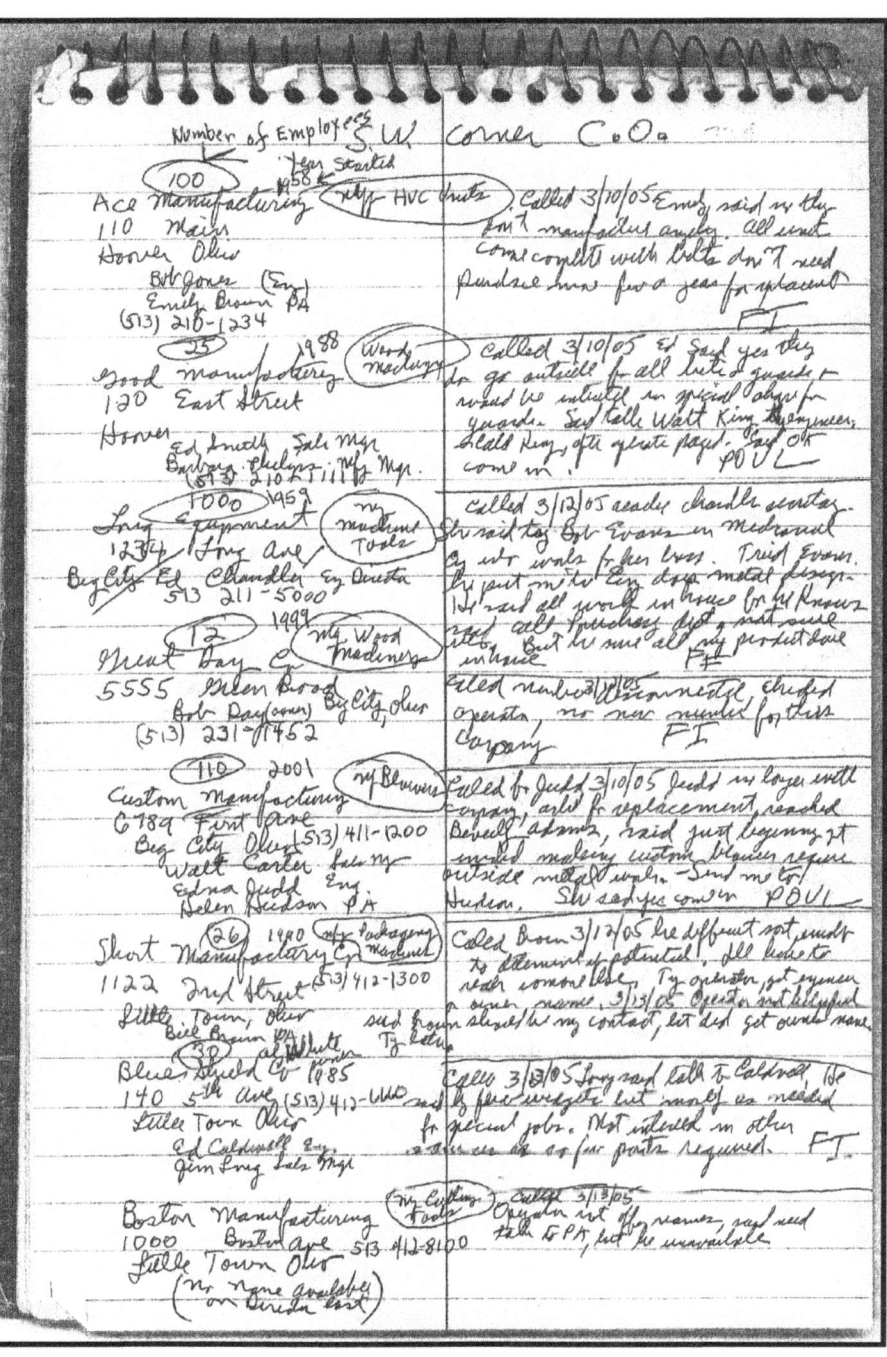

S W Corner   Visit List 3/19/05

(513)   (25)   Good Manufacturing   (Wood Work Machinery From Co.)   Called 3/10/05 ask ... and ryes gr outside to guards Walt King in Eng ... said cousin

2
0
4
1
1
1

120 East Street
Hoover
Ed Smith - called First
Walt King - Eng next appt.
Barbara Phelps PA

(513)   R (110)   Custom Manufacturing   (Mfg Cleaner From Co.)   Adam called 3/10/05 in Eng put me to Hudson. Said come in just starting need outside metal source

4
1
1
2
0
0
D

6789 First Ave
Big City
Beverly Adams   Eng.
Helen Hudson   PA

(513)   R   First Machine Co   (Mfg Pipe)   2/20/05 From called to my manufacturer sent on to me. Do need guards in to walk.

Visited Blue 3/19/05, was prepared with specifics for us to quote. This could be a price check only but need find out so to follow up.

4
1
1
8
0
5

1400 Second St
Big City
Bill Blue

513   R   White Machine Co   Last Visit 7/10/04 Red said we ready start new project Second quarter 05, come back visit. Remind Stainless guard

4
1
1
1
2
6
1

9876 Black St
Red White   Ex 2141

company	A Check Out By Year 05' + Page 1
company	A to Z Roller Co, 2005, pg 19, FI
company	AA Mfg Co., 2006, pg 5, FI
company	AAR Mfg. Co., 2005, pg 9, FI
company	AB Packing Mfg., 2007, pg 13, POVL
company	AB Roller Co., 2009, page 21, open
company	ABL Auto Lift Co. 2006, pg1, FI
company	ACC Aviation Mfg. 2007, pg 28, FI
company	Accurate Distributors, 2005, pg 2, FI
company	Accurate Mfg. Co., 2007, pg 6, POVL
company	Acme Co., 2009, pg 21, FI
company	Action Sales Co., 2006, pg 14, FI
company	Adams Compressor Co., 2006, page 20, FI
company	Advanced Construction, 2009, page 11, FI
company	Advanced Parts Co., 2008, page 9, FI
company	Aero Avenue Distribution, 2008, pg 10, FI
company	Aero Steel Co., 2007, pg 6, FI
company	Aero Zero Mfg., 2008, pg 5, FI
company	Aerospace Industries, 2005, pg11, FI
company	Aerospace Parts Mfg Co., 2009, pg 2, FI
company	AFI Systems Co., 2005, page 11, FI
company	Air True Mfg., 2008, pg 3, POVL
company	Aircraft Specialities, 2008, pg 12, FI
company	Airmack Company, 2005, pg 2, FI
company	All American Machinery 2009, pg 23, FI
company	ALL Systems Co, 2009, page 4, open

Company	A - Visit Records - Ohio	Page 1
Company	A L L Systems, SW pg 2 5/30/05 FI	
Company	AB Packing Mfg.,Cinn, pg 3, 1/4/07, Open	
Company	Ace Mfg, SE pg 2 4/6/07 Opn, 5/3/08 FI	
Company	Air True Mfg , SE pg 9 9/9/08 Open	
Company	Air True Mfg , SE pg1 2/17/05 FI	
Company	B.H.Brecker Co, SW pg 4 3/23/06 FI	
Company	Belcher Dist., SW pg 7 2/21/09 Open	
Company	Berne Tri Mfg, SE pg 12 2/23/04 FI	
Company	Commercial Electric NW pg 9 2/25/08 Open	
Company	D M Mfg Clumbs pg 1 2/13/06 Open	
Company	D R R Co. SW pg 11 3/3/05 FI	
Company	Daniel Company. NC pg 5 4/23/08 Open	
Company	Earl Industries E NC pg 1 3/10/07 FI	
Company	Edge Gear NC pg 2 1/30/04 Open 4/5/06 FI	
Company	Eidmer Distributing. Inc SE pg 4 3/23/06 FI	
Company	Frank Simpson Eng. OC pg 1 1/29/08 FI	
Company	G E B Inc. NW pg 1 3/29/06 Open 5/6/08 FI	
Company	Harris Printer Mfg SE pg 3 3/21/06 Open	
Company	Heilco/Dytn Clumbs pg 10 2/23/05 FI	
Company	Heilco/South Cinn pg 2 2/9/09 Open	
Company	Hoover Engineering SW pg 2 6/27/09 FI	
Company	Howard Mch NW pg 4 3/21/07 Open 9/1/09 FI	
Company	Industry Conveyr Mfg SW pg 10 2/22/05 FI	
Company	Intel Contractors. Cinn pg 7 2/25/07 Open	
Company	J.W.Petro Eng. NC pg 2 3/9/05 FI	

company	**Check Out /Visit List**	**Page 16**
company	Product Mfg Co., co, 2007, pg 5, Fl	
company	Provide Sls Co. vl, IN, Indlps, pg 5, 2009, open	
company	Quick Seal Mfg, co, 2009, pg 3, povl	
company	Quick Seal Mfg, vl, OH, Cinn, pg2, 2009, Fl	
company	Quickn Mfg. vl IN,NE, pg. 5, 7/4/07opn, 8/9/9 Fl	
company	R & P Mach. vl IN NE pg 2, 8/5/08 opn, 8/9/9 Fl	
company	Rink Mg Co.vl OH,SH pg 4, 5/1/7 opn 9/4/9 Fl	
company	Rockwell Div. co, 2005, pg 4, Fl	
company	Rodgers Service Co, co, 2005, pg 4, Fl	
company	Rodgers Tool Co co 2006, Pg 2, Fl	
company	Roll Ben Co. IN, Indlps, vl pg 4, 2007, open	
company	Roll Press Co. co, 2007, pg 11, Fl	
company	Root Drilling Mfg. vl OH, NW pg 4, 2008, open	
company	S A S. Mfg Co. vl, OH, SE, 2008, open	
company	S D L Co co 2005, pg 11, povl, 2009, open	
company	S D Sales Co. vl, OH NW pg 3, 2008, open	
company	Seperation Co, vl IN Indpls pg 6, 2007, open	
company	Services Iron Co co, 2007, pg 7, povl	
company	Services Iron, Co. vl IN, Inds, pg 2, 2009 Fl	
company	Servs Eng. co 2007, pg 7 Fl	
company	Single Shield Mfg, co, 2008 pg 1, povl	
company	Single Shield Mfg, vl, OH, SW pg 6 2008, Fl	
company	Techtonics, co 2008, pg 5, Fl	
company	Thomas Co. co, 2007, pg 2, Fl	
company	Tri Mfg. vl, IN, Inds, pg 2, 2007 opn, 2009, Fl	

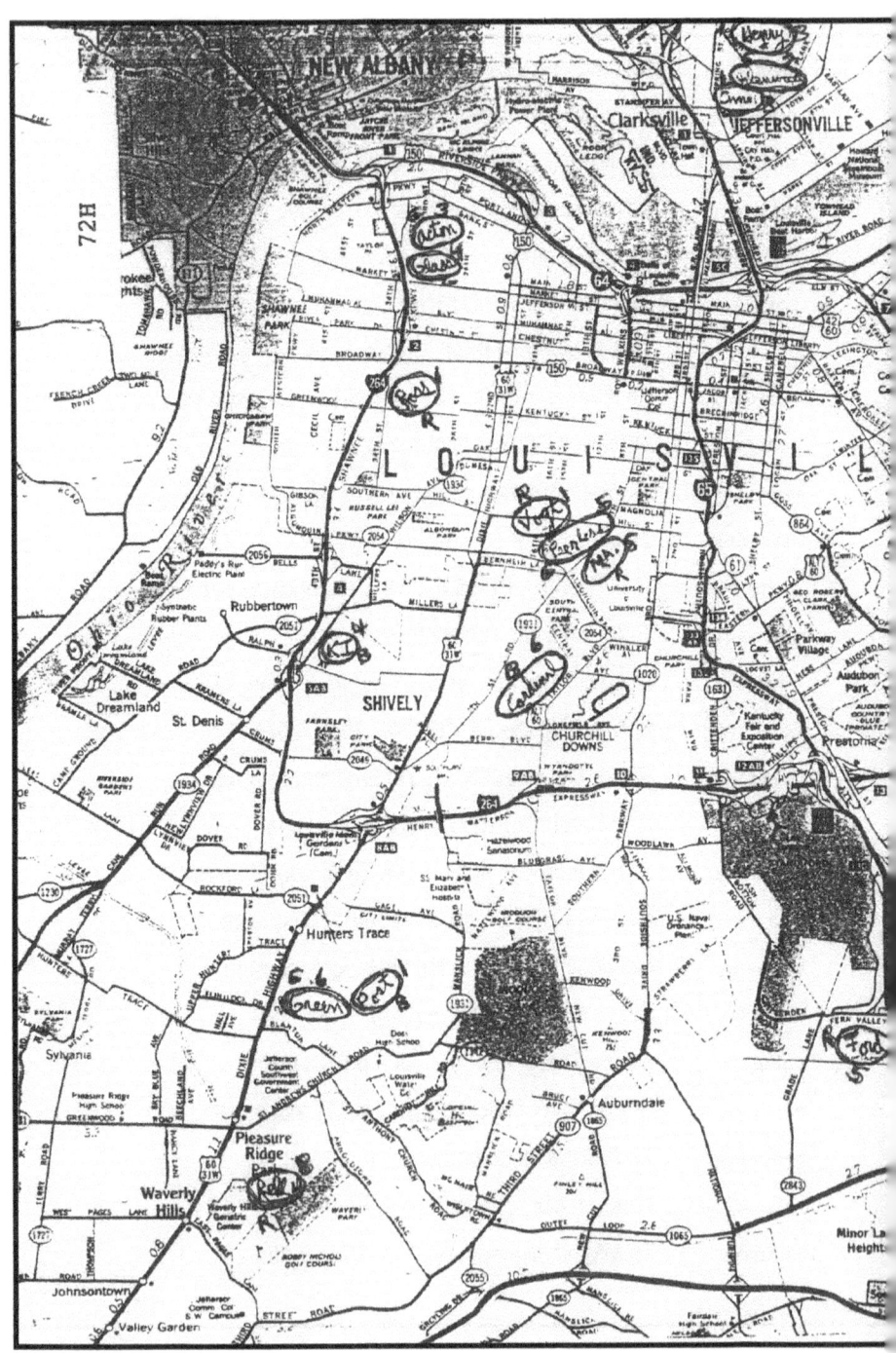

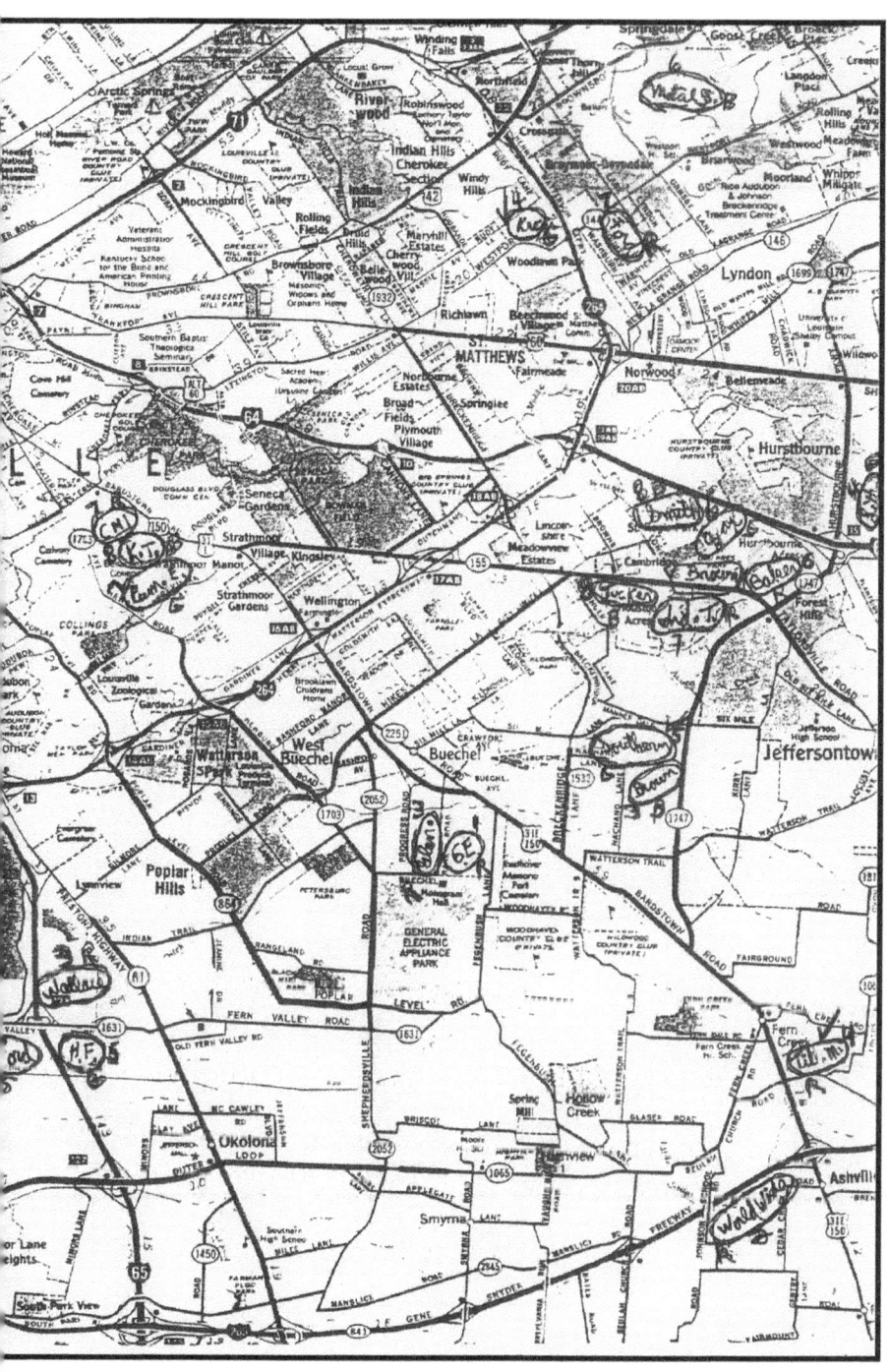

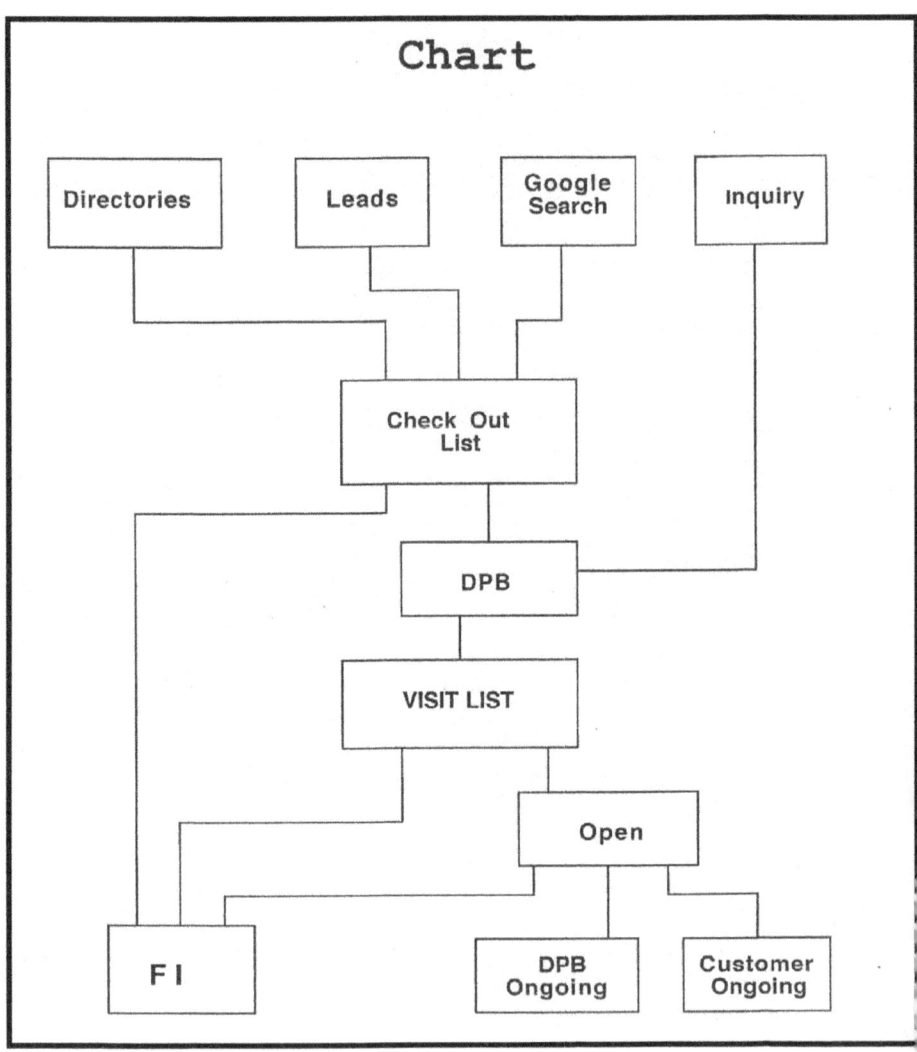

CHAPTER 5

WHO YOU ARE AUGMENTS HOW WELL YOU SELL

get a life lift

Adult communication skill is a day-to-day requirement for salespeople. The precepts that follow can have a lasting impact on your sales experience, and maybe your life too, so listen up.

We've all heard about an errant child that didn't listen to their parents and ended up in trouble, dropping out of school, using drugs and the like. The common response is: why didn't they listen to their parents?—a very involved question, but likely the parents didn't listen to their parents. Sometimes problems stem from parents who don't communicate well with their children, to their plea for recognition, to be heard, to have their opinions count.

If we could magically filter all our elders' garbage, and only assimilate the beneficial things they offer, a lifetime of pain and many regrets could be saved, mistakes avoided, more of the good times enjoyed. Fortunately, most of us have a lifetime to work through our mistakes.

In sales it's different. You have months, maybe a year or two to be successful, no lifetime to reach maturity. So, I've sifted through my sales garbage, and what remains in these pages can give you a lift over everyday sales' hurdles you're certain to encounter. Some of the guidance I offer may seem intrusive at first, but if you think it through and experiment with it in practice, you'll recognize its pecuniary relevance.

I've read an autobiography that helped me a great deal in life. *'In and Out of the Garbage Pail,'* by Fritz Perls. Another of his books, *'Gestalt Therapy Verbatim,'* was somewhat better-known. But unless you were into philosophy and self understanding in the seventies and eighties, you likely missed them. In my opinion Perls was a rather strange fellow, but a definite innovator. He lived an interesting life, and his concepts were at the forefront of learning about changing oneself for the better. He taught knowing oneself for its sake and originated ways that psychiatrists could help patients understand and fulfill themselves. Keep in mind, that fulfillment is the bottom line for this book.

Eric Berne's hypotheses—an author and psychiatrist—were equally important and more well-known. I can rightfully say that Berne's work made my success possible. He developed the theory known as TA, (Transactional Analysis). His book, *'Games People Play,'* although most popular in the sixties and seventies is still in print today, but his *'What Do You Say After You Say Hello,'* is not. You're more likely to have heard of, *'I'm OK your OK'*, a very successful TA book written by Thomas Harris, a protégé of Berne's. It's been said his presentation of TA theory was more easily understood. Harris' book was a best seller, and though I find it dry at times, I recommend it.

The principles of TA are the very essence of honest communication. TA teaches how to communicate on an adult level, to breach our personal emotional responses, and leave that trash behind. This approach is imperative in dealing with customers and fellow employees. Open, adult-to-adult communication, even in the most sensitive circumstances, overcomes most grievances in business and life. Even today, though without recognition, countless sales seminars and self-improvement workshops draw on the concepts that Berne championed. In the last few decades many so-called new ideas for self-improvement are based on Berne's SA (Script Analysis) theories, an expansion of TA. SA delves into parental influences, examining the lifelong hold it perpetuates. Berne was, I'm sure, an innovator whose contributions will affect the human psyche and behavior, as long as we last.

Following are my perceptions of Berne's developments and the life-lift his theories offer, when applied to communication in sales. A method of projecting your thoughts and opinions that will give you a lift above your competition.

Berne's TA divided a person into three ego states, Parent, Adult, and Child. The dictionary's definitions of those words are different from Berne's use of the terms. I'll not delve into TA beyond its sales impact, I suggest reading one of the books mentioned above.

Here's how TA works in sales. The pure adult ego state communicates without intimidation from the other two ego states. The emotion of the child and the judgmental parent are left behind, though it's not easily done. I hasten to add, that the child ego state is the creative one, the one with imagination. We'll need that part of us, too, to sell.

Detrimental early life experiences or stuff we learned from failed parents—that's Script Analysis—are not to be carried into adult decisions or adult communication. They will always be with you in your subconscious, ready to blame, demand, or demean someone, often yourself. In SA, we learn to recognize their detriment and source, and in TA we control the resulting emotions, making it possible to remain in our adult ego state in business communication. When you speak to a client, your boss, or a coworker, the subject can be openly communicated without prejudice to the person or the position of the person you're addressing. Negative tones, facial putdowns, and sarcasm are all learned parent-scripted traits and not part of the adult ego state. Speak your differences from the adult without the garbage of those negative learned experiences. And yes, compliments are positive traits of the adult ego state, a transaction I sometimes have trouble remembering. Using TA principles, the improvement in communication is remarkable. If you remain in your adult state, the subject of your attention can't continue the conversation with their learned garbage of their past, because it takes two for any transaction. TA and SA work wonders in personal relationships, too, but best of all, they expose you to you. Though you might not always like what's revealed, it feels great when you overcome your scripted self, even though it's sometimes only a fleeting moment.

Understanding the payoff for unconscious negative behavior is a complicated psychological circumstance, but certainly left behind in sales.

Adult-focused communication in business is tantamount to success. You ask your production manager, "Is my order for Smith Company going to ship on time?"—an adult transaction.

"Do you think you're the only outside salesperson that's got orders going through here? If I get the time, I'll let you know."

A child response, creating a crossed transaction that goes nowhere and closes any possibility of fruitful conversation, with nothing being accomplished. An adult response would've been; "I'm very busy, but I'll check as soon as possible and let you know." Now, the production manager's response opens the transaction for more adult exchanges.

"Smith is a new customer, and his first delivery could determine if they'll continue ordering from us. It would sure help, if it goes on time."

"Okay, I get it. I'll see what I can do, and try to get back to you today, but I can't promise." The difference in those responses is obvious. Both parties can now approach the subject again at a later time without intimidation.

You'll hear it more than once in these pages: Don't drink and try to sell. Memory and planning are essential, and drinking screws up those perceptions big-time! Thinking on your feet, and quick decisions, are a daily practice. Drinking destroys all the selling essentials, not to mention their birthplace, intellect. I assure you, it doesn't give the lift you're looking for, certainly not the high of landing an important account. Sure, drink, if that's your pleasure, but during personal time. There are professions where drinking is even more precarious. Ever look up at a red-eyed, hung-over surgeon just before you're put to sleep?

This reminds me of a tip an operating room nurse once gave me. It has nothing to do with business sales, but is darn good information. "Don't have surgery on Monday mornings."

It's time for another sidestep, one that's more in keeping with sales. If your sales job requires overnight stays, it can affect your home life, but there are often perks that make up for it. Trips to conventions held at interesting places can include weekends with your spouse. As a manufacturers' agent you can pick and choose trade shows to attend or principals manufacturing facilities to visit. After all, such trips are deductible. A manufacturer in sunny California will have many times the factory visits than one in Buffalo. Sorry, Buffalo!

Traveling is an issue all it's own, and it can wear on you. Here's a number of tongue-in-cheek suggestions that effects sales, too. We all need to be rested before a long day. For sleep sake, insist on following four important hotel rules; go over them while checking in, especially if you're a light sleeper. Your requests are certain to annoy the clerk, who might even look up from the counter to see who you are. Never mind those fidgeting in line behind you; they're not making your mortgage payments. You may encounter unavoidable sleep destroyers, crises that don't occur until you turn off the light.

1. *Never, never* take a room across from or next to the ice or vending machines. Ice banging into a plastic bucket is louder than a cow bell, and the party down the hall will need ice till the wee hours.

2. Be sure your room *is not* near the elevators. The opening and closing doors that ding at each floor won't sing you to sleep. Then, there are rooms that are only divided from a hydraulic elevator shaft by a mere wall. Every up and down of the elevator creates that hydraulic swishing sound. I've memorized numbers of problem rooms in hotels I frequent often. And who is that guy that keeps returning to the floor, cursing loudly each time the elevator door dings open?

3. Next comes a big one, a circumstance that can drive you to the next motel. I recall an instance when I rose at 5:00 AM to catch a plane and after a long tiring sales day reached my hotel by 6:00 PM that evening. The next morning's sales presentation was the most important on the trip, and I desperately needed a good night's sleep. Insist your room *does not* have an adjoining door. The sounds of late-night western movies shoot right through adjoining doors that supposedly separate your life from those next door. That evening I accepted a room with an adjoining door with a promise they weren't busy and the next room would be left unoccupied. 'Yeah, sure!' The couple that checked in

at 2:00 AM argued for several hours, then she cried till near-dawn. Finally it became quiet, but I had only a few hours left to sleep. Suddenly the bed next door creaked those familiar creaks, and through the adjoining door I was serenaded by the usual loud moans and groans. At 7:00 AM I got up, reset the alarm button of my clock to 8:00 A.M., put it on the floor by the adjoining door, showered, dressed, and by 7:45 AM staggered to my 8:30 A.M. meeting. Crass, maybe, but it might make that couple think of other people, when they spend a night in a hotel.

4. Here's a circumstance to avoid that's easily overlooked. *Stay away* from rooms near the stairwell when you're on the second or even the third floor. When elevators are sparse or slow, guests opt to use the stairway, especially if it's near their room. Many stairway fire doors are closed at night, they're heavy and slam closed, as guests scurry down the steps. And there's that guy again, up and down the stairs, mumbling something each time the door bangs behind him.

Unavoidable bad luck can get you anytime. Maybe you've experienced people who talk in the hallway at all hours of the night, unable to tear themselves apart and separate into their own rooms. Short of starting a fight, there's no remedy for rude loudmouths. Then there's the outdoor type, like the guy who works on his car till 3:00 AM just outside your motel room or the diesel truck driver whose engine runs all night. Have you ever wondered where the parents of the kids chasing in the hallways of motels are at night?—likely in the bar. Not much point in calling security on this bunch; it just inspires them.

There is a remedy. If you drive to your destinations, it's easy, take along a fan-driven air purifier. I use an HEPA unit designed to eliminate dust mites, mold, and odor from stagnated air. My purifier provides a pleasant, but loud, fan hum that can drown out the invading noises. Mine has three speed settings, and the highest is perfect for the horny couple next door. If you can't apply the fan noise, follow my other rules. And if I disturbed anyone I apologize, but I must admit I keep forgetting my car keys, my cell phone, my...

If you're lonely on the road and stay in one place for long periods, you can take your pet with you, since they're accepted in many hotels. But be certain not to leave a pet in the car on hot, or even warm, days. I'm sure those with pets are concerned about their well-being, yet some folks are surprised by the pet-conscious persons: those who go out of their way, some a lifetime out of their way, for stray domestic animals. Human neglect created the plight of starving and sick stray domestic animals. You can do your part to make it right. Help in the effort to get animals spayed and neutered, contribute to shelters, then adopt.

My editor suggested taking out the previous paragraph. "Sales... we're talking about a sales career." I was told "Who do you think you are, Bob Barker?" No, I can't come close to Barker's generosity (for those who remember his TV show), but this is an extremely important issue. I'm selling a need, the biggest sale of some animal's life. So, make an effort to learn more. Please, Help out!

CHAPTER 6

FINESSING THE CLIENT
THE MOZART EFFECT

who was that masked salesperson

The customer: With them we sometimes struggle, but without them, well, you know what we are—broke. You might say, a customer to a salesperson is like the bloom to a plant; they're the reason for our growth, yet they exist because we do.

To compile a list of all possible customer types would require a staff of researchers, and that is well beyond the scope of this book. Company selling is actually selling people, so that's what we're dealing with. The oldest sales profession seeks to satisfy customers. And, our selling is just as complex, emotional, and loaded with psychological problems as that one. Remember my scenario of the shoe salesperson at the mall that involved a human factor?

To be truly successful, *one must believe* and practice the following: *The slightest gesture, comment or single action can influence the customer outside the customer's knowledge.* That's finessing. Things like a Christmas gift offered with a sincere, unique comment. Two salespeople could give the same buyer the same bottle of whiskey as a gift, but the person who chooses words that instill, yes instill, good feelings is remembered. For instance, rather than calling a bottle of bourbon, just that, call it a bottle of cheer. Obviously with this example one needs to know the customer's acceptance of alcohol as a gift.

This type of attitude is similar to finessing a sporting activity. Someone accomplishes a difficult feat, because they finesse it. Ever watch tournament water skiing? Both genders need strength to pull themselves through the wakes and around the markers, but women must finesse their skills to match the brute force of men. I've tournament skied and could only watch in awe, as women with much less physical strength far out-performed me.

The opposite of finessing is the person who puts their arm around a customer to express or imply a business kinship, an obvious canned attempt of self-purpose ma-nipulation. (That burns me up, when it's done to me). Remember the Webster definition of manipulation on page 22? I'll repeat it here: "To change by artful or unfair means so as to serve one's own purpose. "We're using the word "artfully" as the interpretation of Webster's explanation of changing someone's thinking.

So here it is, put in sales terms: *To finesse a customer or DPB is to manipulate their thinking and their decision-making outside their awareness. It can be within their awareness, but feels so comfortable one tends to accept it.* In sales when you speak fluently and accurately, you create an art form. You transfer your beliefs to another or in the least, make your convictions clearly available to consider. This action works only when you're convinced the customer or DPB will be better-served with your widget.

All the canned spiels, all the high-power offers and promises aren't as effective as an honest finessed manipulation. Yes, I'll say it again—*honest manipulation.* If you understand this principle and practice it, the skills will become a natural part of your approach and enhance your overall outside sales-life experience. Honest manipulation is a talent with a positive outcome for everyone.

The Ponzi schemes and real estate scams in the late 2000's that wrecked lives and ruined property values for all of us are vivid examples of "unfair" manipulation. And those individuals deserve the wrath of the law. My presentation of honest manipulation is a talent that moves decision-makers toward a favorable conclusion for all.

With that said, some may still find my approach discomforting. They may prefer the words "convince" or "enlighten" when relating how to change a customer's thinking. However, those terms apply to the results achieved. I'm describing the avenue.

Through the years some of the most popular television shows featured honest manipulators. The individuals were portrayed as charismatic, TV trial lawyers attempting to manipulate jurors. The jurors know that the attorney wishes them to believe as they do, to buy what they're offering. But there's a difference in sales, and it favors the lawyer. The jurors are pressed for a decision, guilty or not, yes or no. In sales it's more difficult. Our clients have a third option: Do nothing, stay with the status quo, don't make a decision.

When you can present a new wrinkle, a widget that chimes rather than clanks, or a paint that turns colors with the touch of a button (Man, would that ever sell!), you have an advantage. Finesse it so the decision-maker picks up on the difference themselves, senses the advantage of your product themselves. In a meeting don't rush to explain your widget's advantages, even if you're frothing at the mouth to brag, to expound on how much better it performs than others. Say just enough to allow the customer to make the determination. That's being different, it gets their attention and in sales, unless you have the customer's attention, nothing gets sold.

If you recognize a DPB is already being well-served by a competitor and you don't have a new wrinkle or price advantage, don't push it. Don't, like others do, get into a long boring dissertation about your quality and fast delivery. If the DPB is unhappy with their present vendor for any reason, they'll likely tell you. If they're satisfied with a present source, just let them know you're interested if anything changes. It's okay to tell them how you believe your company fits with their requirements. Be personally impressive by being yourself. Use adult-to-adult communication skills. Finesse your delivery and leave it at that. Remember The Lone Ranger? Hi-yo Silver away! Even out of sight, after finessing your sales comments, you'll be remembered when the present vendor screws up, goes out of business, or encounters other problems all manufacturers, distributors and service companies face. Always check back. I have seen totally unexpected things happen to competitors that change the thinking of a DPB, and sometimes in weeks.

Know the inside details about the DPB. The best finesse hasn't a chance, if the customer's daughter is your competitor. If the decision-maker is family connected to a competitor, don't waste your time. DO, and this is a big DO, stay in touch. That family member may change jobs or move away, and the product that customer didn't really favor in the first place will soon be history. You should be in touch often enough, so that you get first chance when all things are equal again. Be sure the PA you've decided to go around is not the sister of the owner; that happened to me, and boy, did it cause me problems!

There are times when the customer is connected in other ways that create problems. The toughest and most exasperating is graft; it's quite rare, but still out there, so I'll mention it. Because it's your time invested, you serve as the jury in those decisions, but with no power to commute a sentence, other than to walk away. Once, years ago, I had a buyer ask me for two expensive tickets to a baseball game. I had bypassed him, getting my motors specified by engineering. He had no choice except to buy from me. So, he set me straight. Yes, I did get him those tickets, but someone else blew the whistle on him and he was retired. He'd apparently been enriching himself, using the purchasing department for over 30 years.

Enhancements like football season tickets or an expensive TV are too much for either to be considered a reasonable Christmas gift, but not enough to be considered criminal. Many large companies restrict gifts of any sort, especially those companies who manufacture and sell to the US Government. Nowadays they better!

Finessing the customer is a creative art. Remember the remarks I made about selling your mate on a product you want? Where did the ideas come from, and how did you come up with your plan? It's like composing music. Moods, thoughts, even conclusions are born of the creative child in us all. I call it *The Mozart Effect*. Mozart once said, speaking of his ideas for composing music, "Whence and how they come, I know not, nor can I force them."

Imagination can work for you, too. You're on the way to see the next DPB, but before you drive away, you review your written comments from the last few visits with the person you're heading to see. Along the way you reminisce about those visits: Think about the upcoming encounter; envision the last conversation and the objections to using your widget; think about the person, their product; picture their face; hear their voice, then let it happen. Don't push it, The Mozart Effect works on its own.

You may think of a line of conversation that will lead the customer to initiate conversation about the widget you're seeking to highlight; that's finessing. Don't do comparisons, avoid running down the competition, or you'll imply the customer's stupid for selecting that widget in the first place. Don't add anything further. Concentrate on your product, always ignore the shortcomings of your competition. An RFQ is likely. Above all, don't repeat yourself; that's boring. Boring and outside sales mix like oil and water.

Finessing works, unfortunately, I can hear the objections of many longtime salespeople, "That stuff's too complicated, it's not necessary to be so word mindful."

"Oh yes, it is!" When you open your mind to the music of finessing, when you allow your thoughts to surf your mind's Internet, the Mozart effect will create images of your forthcoming conversation with a customer, and most important, give birth to new proposals that make your product stand out. You *will* see yourself with the customer. Imagine the results when he or she says exactly what you hoped for. Mozarts happen to me in all sorts of places: Long walks, driving on the expressway, cutting grass.

Developing accounts through creative thinking is the backbone of outside sales success. Finessing separates you from the sales stooge, a person who repeats the same monotonous sales pitch at each stop. "Best price, best service, go forward with us" Can you imagine how many times those words are uttered? If you're an ex-PA now considering a sales career, you already know about tiresome people, and that knowledge gives you a definite advantage. Give your imagination time to create words that artfully and honestly manipulate a

DPB into seeing your point, ultimately, even making it for you.

We're all unique individuals and that's what gets attention, maybe even startles a customer. Being yourself, being truthful, is unique, you gain the confidence of a DPB when you present your widget honestly and without airs; it comes back to getting one's attention. If you've seen the same movie many times (canned comments), you tend to be disinterested. Watch out, if you notice a bored reaction when speaking to a DPB, you'll know, you've, strayed too.

There's a problem side to being yourself when you buck what's considered the acceptable social majority, and it can be a bumpy road, but that's to be expected. The pluses, the experiences, the satisfaction far outweigh "doing it like everyone else."

French philosopher, mathematician and scientist, René' Descartes 1596-1650 said in his famous phrase, "I think, therefore I am." If you remember only one part of this chapter, remember this: It's very basic. You're likely to quickly say, "Well, of course," and without examining it carefully not get the full effect. It's this: People do react to what you say. *However, humans are all very different and they react differently to the same stimuli. Know who you're addressing!*

Tell your spouse you cheated, what happens? You get shot? They leave? They ask what they did wrong? Maybe get turned on and ask to hear the details, while tearing at your clothes. Humans can be weird.

One DPB can be provoked to anger by the same question that might make another think twice about selecting one of your competitor's products. A good example of an ill-informed question: "How many cycles does your machine complete until the widget malfunctions?" If you already know your competitor's widget failure is premature, *and the DPB knows you know*, then asking that question is like the "arm-around" tactic, an obvious ploy.

Consider what I'm professing. Think through each encounter as you write (compose) your next Visit List. Make a note, when something strikes you while you reminisce over past visits. Always make notes, even when thoughts hit you in the shower, write it down the moment you step out. Henry Ford once said, "Ideas are like quail; once in flight they are gone forever."

Images are often sparked driving to the next sales visit. Turn your attention to the beautiful day, the park you're driving by, the sound of birds chirping. If it's not that kind of neighborhood, you may have to take inspiration from the graffiti, obscene paintings, and personal memorabilia painted on the boards covering windows of deserted buildings. In either case let your mind sparkle, while the billions of synaptic junctures send impulses through your brain and somehow, some way, new creative thoughts give birth to just the perfect comment for the right customer. As Mozart said, "All this fires my soul, and provided I am not disturbed, my subject enlarges itself, becomes methodized and defined, and the whole, though it be long, stands almost complete and finished in my mind, so that I can survey it, like a fine picture, a beautiful statue, at a glance."

CHAPTER 7

THE WRITTEN WORD

tools and hammers

Creative written words will get you noticed. Mightier than the sword? History differs, but it works here.

There are so many standard salutations and quote formats, it would serve no purpose for me to offer more. Obviously, the technical portions of letters, e-mail, and quotes should be addressed without wasting words. Proofreading a document once or twice before it's sent usually reveals repetition and unnecessary phrases.

Managers, listen up. The following is crucial, because it can get salespeople to DPB decision-makers, where other exercises fail. Be sure you get the necessary departments to cooperate, especially where the salesperson doesn't prepare the written quote. However, regardless of the quote originator, the salesperson involved should have the opportunity to review quotes going into their areas. Salespeople in the field can be

e-mailed drafts. If quotes are everyday part number requirements the preview is not usually necessary. What's
next obviously doesn't apply to existing customers, and
not all DPBs, but it works.

Let's say you're quoting a series of widgets to an
important DPB's drawing. Have your engineering or
quotations department offer the parts in a way that
exceeds what the DPB expects, beyond what's seen
every time they have these parts quoted. Look for some
opening in their documents, a way to offer a suggestion
or improvement. Don't ask if it's okay to quote with an
extra slant as an alternate, just do it. The "JUST DO
IT" phrase is about worn out, but it's an important fit
here. If possible quote in a way that enhances their part
or offers an alternative with a price advantage.

Include an option with a MECHANICAL VARIATION
that improves the item, or a husky discount that
requires a TECHNICAL DEVIATION to the PA's RFQ.
Approval of either will normally demand the involvement
of engineering, management, or maybe just the next
person up the chain. Remember, getting your name to
additional people, getting their names, getting them
involved, and meeting decision-makers leads to sales.
This procedure is equally important, because you can
verify that the inquiry for your quote is authentic, not
a run-around. You'll also have a legitimate reason to
follow up the quote with the new name.

Maybe you or others within your company who
prepare or provide material for written quotes could
suggest a production change by eliminating an
unnecessary machining operation that saves money,
but also requires approval of a key individual.

Offering an entirely different product to do the same
job, can be an interesting twist to a DPB.

Now comes an important procedure for the
salesperson. When a quote is completed, look it over
carefully, let your imagination see the words and
numbers like the customer or the DPB might see them.
Leave it on your desk, store it as a draft, don't rush to

send it, let it sit overnight, even two nights if possible. Seeing your own work in the morning is having the best editor available. Allow the Mozart in you to emerge. Maybe a word or phrase can be added or the numbers rearranged to make your point more appealing. Your written work should always get their attention, whether hard copy or e-mail. If you give the Mozart in you time to compose, you'll have an advantage over those who don't believe.

There's another set of circumstances we need to cover. Quoting your widget or anything that doesn't have *an equal,* may provoke immediate attention and concern. Many companies stay clear of single sourcing. Oftentimes it can't be helped. Such is the case where a large outlay for initial tooling or engineering time is required or the product was difficult to manufacture, requiring time to sort through quality concerns. It happens when architects, consulting engineers, or contractors select single source products. These circumstances add additional long-term performance responsibilities to the vendor. When it's up front, this kind of marriage is something to be achieved, setting up a long-lasting monetary association.

Commodity items such as paper, steel, and plastics, to name a few, may fall in the Internet purchase category. Great! In that circumstance outside salespeople solicit those buyers too. Nothing new!

Some large companies are reducing their supply and vendor numbers in order to eliminate paper contamination. However, I think that approach is subject to change, depending on the comings and goings of large company CEO's. Out-source purchasing management companies are hired to replace corporate purchasing functions, taking over many sourcing roles. Their criteria: reduce the number of vendors, and written quotes. Salespeople can step up to the plate. If agreeable to all parties—and try to make it so—letters, faxes, e-mails and all forms of quotes sent to the out-source purchasing company, should be copied to the customer, or DPB insuring accountability. It's not a threat to the out-source company, but it could guarantee your company remains in the mix if the out source provider changes.

The written word is a powerful force. You realize an important advantage about your widget and you verbalize it to a DPB during a sales visit. They're impressed for the moment, maybe an hour. A letter, fax, or e-mail gives that same comment decisive significance. A brief written confirmation a week after an important sales visit is a great tool. Time between the visit and the written follow-up is adjustable as required. A fax usually works well, as long as you know the message is delivered. E-mail works, but only if you know the e-mail habits of your addressee. So many Internet messages are flying around, some people don't take time to sort through them and spam gobbles up communications too.

If you have an important visit scheduled, one that requires traveling, especially if it includes arranging for others to participate, always send a written confirmation a week or so before the visit. Always! Don't waste the fire power of an expert from your company with a misunderstood or forgotten appointment. Unfortunately, even writing can't assure your message about an appointment will be remembered. One can always say, "Didn't see a letter/fax/e-mail." So, even after sending a hard copy or e-mail, also re-phone that particular client who previously missed an appointment.

A word on business traveling companions. As an agent I picked those times carefully. There are specific circumstances where the impact of a traveling companion presented as an expert, a direct voice of authority from production, can have a lasting beneficial effect. When you're on the fence with a company, within inches of having them change from their past supplier to you, your traveling companion from the plant can provide the impetus for the change. Perhaps someone behind the scenes needs convincing, someone you rarely have an opportunity to reach. Through your normal channels with purchasing, suggest an exchange of engineering expertise or use your traveling expert's title. "General Manager" has a nice ring to it. If you need to reach a maintenance person, your own maintenance engineer would sound imposing. Remember, put details of the visit in writing, with copies to all parties. However, like everything else, if it's overdone, it loses its flavor. *"Too much mustard ruins the beans."*

It's wise to suggest your traveling companion send written thanks to the people you visited together. Even if the visit doesn't require follow-up work, a note of thanks for their time will be remembered. It's especially effective if they go to the trouble to mail the thanks.

Carefully thought-out memos, e-mail, fax, or letters to internal persons within your own company about a new order from a new customer can oftentimes assure on-time shipments. If it's a first order, your company is being tested, so be sure everyone within your company knows the opportunity presents many dollars of future business. Include a copy to an important person (management) within your company. In other words, use the written word to keep everyone within your company on their toes. It should be added that you shouldn't abuse the first order situation. It's the old story of "crying wolf"; don't do that. Still worse, never put yourself in the position of saying after the fact, *"If only I had written a memo to Maurice in production, and copied my boss."*

I've included an actual letter I wrote to the engineering department of my Principal who brushed off a nonspecific inquiry from my customer. Had my company not responded, and they did after my letter, they would've lost credibility with the customer. My own engineering department didn't want to take time to respond to the customer's engineer, partly because management within my company intently scrutinized engineering time.

I'd sent my engineer what gear drawings and sketches the customer had developed. "I can't quote with that information," my engineer complained. "The price could be anywhere. It would take valuable engineering time to make his sketches quotable, and I've got other inquiries to handle." An okay adult comment, leaving me a response.

"Perhaps," I answered. "But experience tells me tooling and prototypes can be priced from similar past gear designs. Since you're quoting gears every day, you certainly can get closer than me. What similar jobs have you processed?" I insisted.

The customer's concept could replace gears altogether. I wanted our engineer to explore an alternative that still used gears, just a different concept. Expressing interest to a customer's question is important with an existing account, not to mention the damage a competing gear company could do helping this engineer. Once again the outside salesperson must push it through and get it done. My engineering would've left it at, "Sorry, I can't help with this one." I could have dropped the subject after complaining verbally, but my words would have been useless. The written word works wonders.

If you've been in sales for a while, I'm sure you've been frustrated by inter-company indifference at some point; it does happen. If you write a e-mail, memo, or fax to your inside contact, whether they're in engineering, production, quality control, shipping, etc., stating you've sent it for the record, they'll realize it's in their professional interest to act. Their job would be at stake if your company lost an account following a written request they ignored. You must be resolute, and the written word makes the best impression.

The following fax is a replica of the original, except I've changed the names and dates to protect the guilty.

As an employee of a company you may have to temper your comments as opposed to my position as a manufacturers' agent; then again, if you're the brave sort, maybe not.

FAX

April 1, 2500

Aloysius VanStallarocystuch
Northern Machine Company
1111 South Cloud 9
Someplace 000000

Ref: Listen Corporation

Dear Aloysius,

Your response to my telephone call regarding Listen Corporation
did not consider all the ramifications beyond the moment.

We enjoy their business today because of my persistence with
their engineering during the time the present designs were
evolving. (That engineer has since moved on.) I have met with
and talked to the latest engineer, Lou Needhelp, several times.
He requires outside assistance to develop a new generation of
gearboxes. His opinions will impact decisions on manufacturers of
future gears. We need him on our side.

It is clear you cannot devote extensive engineering dollars to
sketches, but to ignore his request (he had taken time to present
me with a number of documents), for ballpark prices is a mistake.
Just a little of your time to demonstrate Northern Machine's interest
in his project will pay off in the future. To say it could cost anywhere
in the thousands, could be $2,000 or $50,000.

Please approach this request a bit more carefully. The question
again: What kind of cost as a gear manufacturer do you envision
will be involved? Tooling, prototypes, production costs, what can
you give him? Quantities are 50 to 200 yearly. Please call me first,
if you decide to phone him before a written estimate.

Thanks,

Walter Nussbaum Jr.

cc: Bill Getitdone, President, Northern Machine Co.

The point made here occurs elsewhere in these pages, BUT IT'S NOT REPETITIVE, WHEN THE SAME ANSWER FOLLOWS DIFFERENT QUESTIONS.

The written word seals the deal. Make written notes, especially and get them to your Visit List. If you remember a comment that will improve a telephone call, write a note. Interrupt whatever else you're doing, even if it takes five minutes to write standing at the kitchen counter, while your cat stalks your steak; hide it from her. A high cabinet is a great place to hide your dinner from the cat.

When visiting with a customer, I always carry a small memo pad, and when follow-up procedures are required, I write it in the presence of the customer, tear out that page, and put it in my top pocket to transfer to the appropriate place. The memo was there, making that noise crinkled paper makes, each night when I removed my shirt. Maybe it was just to send the person I was visiting a brochure, magazine clipping, or whatever I'd promised. I didn't leave it to memory. I always compiled a TTD (Things To Do) list after every day of business. Notes made with electronic devices that won't allow you to forget would work, too, but using those devices can't always be done discretely in the presence of the DPB. Notes and more notes—this book includes a conglomeration of them.

Written reports of meetings or inspections at job sites are needed in document form. Letters or e-mails should be brief and direct. Brief, is also best for solicitation letters, either individual or form. When it's appropriate, an entertaining comment now and then gives written business communication a personal touch. Remember, avoid the "arm around" action. When you're writing a defensive report or letter, one that deals with your company screw-ups, be factual, don't slant it in either direction. Above all be sure your communication recognizes the complaints that have been registered by the customer, and it's important that you, the writer, acknowledge you understand the problem. Write a letter or e-mail to your boss and/or your production department, outlining the problems and your efforts to date, but don't harp on your company's mistakes.

An example sent to your boss might read "...there is no need to repeat the circumstances of the failure, as they're well understood, now we must..." Make suggestions to correct what's wrong. Whenever possible, include copies of your inter-company communications to the customer. That gesture will be remembered and assure confidence in the integrity of your company.

Employment contracts that you're asked to sign are written documents that need close attention. Don't be overly cautious about asking questions. If your questions provoke problems, that in itself is valuable information, when considering employment. If you feel the need, put your questions in writing. Don't be intimidated. Go with your gut feelings. With those attitudes, you're likely to be considered an individual with determination, one with a sense of fair play that's seeking and offering long term commitment.

CHAPTER 8

LOOK WHAT I BROUGHT HOME
CAN WE KEEP IT

everybody's an expert

You may be faced with individuals within your company that decide, without basis, they're a sales expert. Though this chapter could be disarming to some, I would be remiss not including it. Maintaining customers in the face of overbearing peers requires dedication. This is a tough situation for the newcomer, but with the right balance it's something you can control. Management should approach this chapter with an open mind.

Next, let's look at two episodes of the long-standing question: "What could be worse than that?"

At the last instant, just before she opens the door, you remember your blind date's name and then see that she *is* someone you dated before, but had forgotten.

What could be worse than that? Answer: Looking directly at you, she has no idea who you are.

What could be worse for a salesperson than the management of their company knowing little or nothing about outside sales? What could possibly be worse than that? Answer: Management that knows little or nothing about outside sales, BUT think they do.

I've had first hand experience with unqualified sales experts. A plant manager at a large international manufacturing company purchased a small manufacturing company and I was his first representative. He was a manufacturing whiz, but thought sales knowledge was automatic. After several tumultuous years he acquiesced when my small territory grew to represent a large percentage of his overall business. Had I been a salaried salesperson, it would have been over before it began.

It's important as a salesperson to understand a customer's or DPB's opinions and attitude when you submit a quote. If others prepare your quotes you may ask for certain details that don't appear important to inside personnel. Thereby a quote's prepared as usual to move quickly to the next inquiry. A quote may not be competitive only because it was done in haste or didn't address the salesperson's issues, and what you ultimately hoped to accomplish with the style of quote requested. Communicate your reasoning; ask again if needed. Remember the last chapter. It explained how quoting a product with a mechanical variation can get a DPB's attention.

If your outside sales success depends on your company hierarchy, and you're lucky enough to work with all good inside people, you're fortunate, very fortunate. Go to their office and personally thank them. If you have to fight your way through management to get the job done you can still be highly successful, maybe with ulcers, and high blood pressure, but successful still.

The intricacies of handling customers is a way of life for the outside salesperson. Without management recognition of the outside salesperson's efforts, confrontation may develop.

Once again I refer to Webster's Dictionary. "Confrontation": The clashing of forces or ideas. To be a highly successful salesperson, you must become acquainted with this word, as it will be part of your world. Most people shy away from confrontation. There are those that depend upon our doing just that. Some people, groups, companies, rely on the public being weary of confrontation for their very existence. You make a mistake buying a used boat and you know that the dealer becomes easily irritated. He counts on his dissatisfied customers being intimidated by his strong aggressive response. The massive company that threatens your property with a zoning change expects you to avoid confrontation. They make it easy for you not to confront them by using verbal promises about environmental constraints they don't plan to keep. We all know the threatened feeling those situations create.

"What's that got to do with sales?" one might ask. My answer: The intent of this book is to acquire and maintain customers, even though the actions required aren't always a science. The human psyche is an important consideration in sales.

In selling, confrontations with others in your company is likely. If you avoid it, you're not giving your customer, or DPB, the attention demanded. Look at confrontation as just another challenge—another competition. Prepare yourself as you might for a sports event. The tougher the competition the better you'll play. That's the attitude necessary in outside sales, and that goes for the disagreeable PA that keeps you from getting to the decision-maker. Just be careful and know your limits, unless, of course, you've decided getting kicked out of a lobby is no worse than no business.

Over the years I've had sales people, engineering types and production people tell me, "Yes, yes, I talked to the customer... no problem." They explain the customer was perfectly happy with the quote, the late delivery, and/or their explanation of a product failure, all the while implying with a demeaning tone, "You must have exaggerated the customer's reaction."

As the outside salesperson you can't leave the customer's objection rest at that juncture, as the problem would, in fact, disappear along with the account. When possible avoid this perplexing entanglement and address customer problems yourself. That's easily done selling for small manufacturers. Unfortunately, in today's company hierarchies handling customer problems yourself is often difficult or next to impossible. Keep your cool, do your job, and keep the customer. Hopefully your company management will appreciate your diligence.

Tactfully make the point that customers respond differently to management, or others within your company than to you, the outside salesperson. Explain that customers don't want to burn their bridges and therefore won't complain to management, but once they're confident they can replace your product, they're gone. Remind them that if you're right, and if they, your company, doesn't comply with your particular request to keep the customer happy it could cost you the account.

Not wanting to be wrong among peers or to be blamed for losing a customer is a biggie. A memo or e-mail about your customer concerns will almost always gets action, but weigh the plus and minus carefully. Write the report from the adult ego state without being antagonistic. No need to encourage further hostile action. Always avoid "Got'cha" and all its demeaning cousins. When competent management care as you do about sales a short meeting with involved individuals in the boss's office usually works wonders.

Here's an example of management cooperation. Traveling with my electric motor Principal's plant manager, a rare occurrence, I took him on an unannounced visit with a customer experiencing problems with roller bearings in our special designed electric motors. The decision-maker PA and electrical engineer were away, whereby the reason I didn't have an appointment. However, I still wanted to take advantage of my companion's know-how and authority. Loading constraints and lubricants were involved, and worse, the customer's politics enhanced the problem. We got into the plant through the mechanical engineer. I knew he was outside the electric motor decision loop, but for some reason he buddied up to my visiting plant manager. He wanted to impress my companion with his expertise, assuring him that he had the motor bearing problem in hand and nothing needed doing. I couldn't let this rest. The PA was the person who needed to be convinced we could in-fact correct the motor bearing failures. He had been considering a competitor whom I knew had a price advantage.

Before we left the plant, I was able to persuade my plant manager of the critical nature of the problem, explaining to him I knew the personality of the customer's hierarchy. *He accepted my evaluation* as the salesperson involved, took careful notes, and followed up with manufacturing adjustments at the plant. Later, I explained the details of the fix to the PA in the presence of an electrical engineer and they agreed the problem would be corrected. Therefore, once again, the salesperson pushed it through and got it done. Influencing my plant manager was a *completely hidden event* that saved a six-figure account. As a manufacturers' agent my interest was the resulting commission. A salaried outside salesperson should write a detailed visit report and send it to necessary personnel.

Management should be responsive to the outside salesperson's decisions and advice about customers; the ins and outs. Don't be tenuous or you'll lose accounts and worse, lose self-assertive salespeople.

You have to decide: Is your hierarchy more important than the customer? Trust the judgment of the outside salesperson even if some requests are borderline. You might respond, "We already use a team concept."

That's good, but try something bold. *Make the outside salesperson pivotal, with supporting departments accountable to her/ him. Also, if the outside salesperson reports directly to, or has the option to reach the boss, and others know that fact, you'll have an overall increase in teamwork.*

Companies of twenty or fewer people are unlikely to have teamwork problems. The owner is usually the sales manager. You can be sure every employee in such companies are responsive to sales.

Doing things too quickly also jeopardizes customers in other ways. Sometimes internal responses on delivery questions are voiced from memory without verification, but giving the impression it was checked. I had an electric motor plant supervisor try that with me whenever I called him after 4:00 PM. I will add again that an *outside salesperson that cries wolf* on all delivery schedules provokes bad chemistry between inside and outside people. As an outside salesperson you need to make an ally of inside sales, not alienate them. In fact, sometimes inside sales must face confrontation within their own company's hierarchy. In any case, there are few problems when everyone is conscientiously pushing to get the job done. I work with people like that everyday.

It's a fact: A new account a salesperson's been grooming for a long time can be lost by a mere word or a disgruntled tone by someone on the inside; an e-mail brush-off, or even a bored response by an operator; it happens, and you better believe it or some outside salesperson who's been waiting for that first order after exhaustive efforts will be looking for that inside perpetrator with daggers in their eyes, and bills for back-to-school clothes in their pockets.

Another sales problem: That small and inconsequential first-order you finally get from a possible large customer with big future potential is intentionally delayed by production behind other orders of greater value. Make everyone aware why a small order is important, and what's needed to *keep this customer.* Communicate your reasoning to anyone involved, but don't depend on e-mail in-order to avoid confrontation. Some people read e-mails with such haste the messages make little impact. When it's first order important, go see the person, find them in the plant, or phone. I've been lucky to work with shop personnel that listen to my pleas. *Again, be resolute, but no crying wolf.* The first-order problem is most troubling during strong business economies. Management can lose sight of the value of establishing new business by just staying ahead of current orders. When the economy swings the other way and orders decline, interest in new business is renewed, sometimes too late.

Here's a weird human trait: It could happen that the *customer's* purchasing department will discount the salesperson's initiative. I've heard that complaint through the years from salespeople I've known. It's always a topic of conversation at trade shows. I think it has something to do with a conception that the salesperson's efforts diminish the involvement of the buyer, or other requisition departments. If the discount filters back to the salespersons boss that salesperson must be willing to set the record straight and I can't overstress that point.

There are those that think products sell themselves. Listen closely managers. Internal conflicts are born and accounts lost, because self-appointed sales experts attempt to deflate the impact of the outside salesperson.

Here's a perfect example with a kicker at the end. A very large potential account, a company of 1000 employees, had been the subject of my extensive efforts for electric motor sales for years. I won't detail all the strategy involved, but some background is required.

I'd seen purchasing, and though my product had a technical advantage, my pricing was no better than the present source, so their hands were tied. The PA always reminded me engineering must be convinced my electric motors were better-suited for their machines. However, engineering was happy with the present motors, and that was in spite of the fact that my products had a unique advantage. Their key people didn't want to be bothered. I went to their chief engineer, who agreed there were advantages, but to use my motors required changes to their machines, and machine redesigns fell to those that didn't want the extra work. I went back and forth countless times, eventually making my way to marketing. Though they agreed my product improved theirs, company politics blocked their efforts.

It took many months to arrange a meeting, but I took my plea to their export manager. BINGO! His interest was so keen, he went to the chief engineer himself, insisting they take a look. He told the company president about his interest and let engineering know he'd talked to their CEO. Engineering was forced to consider the changes required in their machines to use my motors. Eventually, my motors became the impetus for an improved design of their machine. I was so despised by the customer's purchasing and engineering departments that when motor shipments began, they directed orders to a sister-company of my manufacturer to avoid buying through me. However, that was okay, as I received credit when the motors were invoiced to the sister-company (luckily also in my territory). Later, another engineer was appointed to head up the new machine, and we got along fine. Purchasing wised up and placed their orders with my Principal. The entire episode took years to evolve. There were countless meetings coordinating designs, and even heated arguments with my own people for special parameters.

Now for the kicker! An engineer with the company I represented came on the scene, and offered this observation, and I'll try to quote him verbatim: "Walter Nussbaum, would like you to believe he was responsible for this business, but we have it because of the unique design of our motors."

Once again, as a manufacturers agent, that statement didn't change anything for me. I got my commission. Congratulations for a sale is unnecessary for a manufacturers' agent, just show them the money. However, for a salaried salesperson that shortsighted comment could cause serious internal problems. See—make notes of your efforts, write memos, e-mails, establish a paper trail! The comment came from an engineer whom I had worked with for some time. He was a good guy, and a sharp engineer, but lacked experience in the daily grind the outside salesperson negotiates.

Don't misunderstand. It's not my intention to create walls between outside salespeople and inside counterparts (sales, engineering, management, or peripheral departments). I'm stripping away the covering, the foliage that hides the wall. Only then can you follow the advice of Chapter Five, and use adult-to-adult communication!

As my encounter testifies, human ingenuity in outside sales proves its value. Getting product information to a hidden decision maker, and guiding the process throughout that customer's hierarchy is a big part of creative selling. *You initiate ways of selling what others design and manufacture,* and that's why successful salespeople are paid to be the cutting edge. You can't escape it; at every level salespeople produce the need for other jobs.

The engineer's remark reminds me of a personal encounter I've never forgotten, where another salesman's efforts were being discounted. So, I'll digress and share a personal story, one that demonstrates the importance of inspiration in selling.

Whenever I travel to St. Louis, I stay at an old, renovated hotel near the Union Train Station which has been converted and houses shops and restaurants. On one particular morning, I'd just returned from the hotel breakfast bar to my table with a second doughnut and cup of tea. The ambiance of the old hotel, once the home of St. Louis railroad workers in the early 20th century, may have influenced my perception of what was to unfold. Now a Drury Inn, the hotel lobby is refurbished in its original flavor. It was early morning, and the lobby was almost empty. High on the walls old trains and groups of drab-dressed unsmiling railroad workers peered down at me from large framed pictures. I could feel the eerie presence of the people from that nostalgic era.

Though they had many options, two men with breakfast in hand settled near me, each was taking credit for a record sale from the previous day. They agreed only that their local outside salesman, who had wooed the new customer for some time, had little to do with their closing the sale. To overcome a strong compulsion to approach them, I moved to another section.

Then something strange happened. I sat close to an elderly woman, likely in her late eighties, seated alone in the lobby. The years had inflicted their toll on her body. Her shoulders were stooped from the pain of arthritis. I can still visualize her expression, much like that of my late grandmother, whose bright eyes and warm smile manifested a pride and self-confidence I've rarely seen in the youngest of people. Her gestures were assuring, seemingly reacting to the words of some invisible person seated across from her at the small table. She spoke quietly in return, her words almost indistinguishable to me. One young couple passing to the breakfast bar lingered to stare. She conceded to them briefly, and they moved away.

Not long after, she stood and crossed the lobby to the elevator. From my table I watched her every movement until the elevator door closed me from her life. I was spellbound. I tore a page from a steno pad for a permanent record of my impressions of that moment, and wrote:

The elderly woman's charisma captured my attention. She sat alone in the hotel lobby chatting to an empty space across the table.

She looked knowingly at passersby who expressed pity in their glance. "I'm not mad," she exclaimed to a young couple who paused to gawk. "He left this earth recently, so why not speak my thoughts aloud? For all you know, he may be sitting just there," she said, motioning to an empty chair.

The couple's faces flushed, their hands clasped tightly, and they moved quickly away.

The old woman turned; her gaze fixed across the table, an understanding smile crossed her face. "They're young," she said. "I wish them a life as full as ours."

A sigh, not her own, was faintly discernible.

"Did I really hear that?" I asked myself. I shook the spell that possessed me, finished my tea, and folded the steno page into my pocket. Inspired by the woman in the lobby I headed for my first sales visit. Later, after a tedious day, I found the paper, reread my comments, and felt my tension subside. To this day that memory intrigues me. Inspiration is a stimulant. It surrounds you; use it.

If you're asking yourself why would I want a career in outside ICBBS with confrontations and all the hurtles, well, it's good that you understand the pluses and minuses. *Airline pilots train for unexpected catastrophes, even though they're rarely, if ever, called upon to handle them; the same applies to some of the lessons in this book.* In addition, there is personal satisfaction and highs that aren't possible with many jobs. Keep reading your rewards are coming up.

CHAPTER 9

WINNERS NEVER CROSS
THE FINISH LINE

are you ready for success

What's better than having a valuable, dependable account; where the business is steady and/or growing; where your products or services are capable of continued satisfaction for the customer; where your relationship with the decision maker(s) are stable; where a mutual respect exists between your companies; where your manager pats you on the back, while handing you your bonus check. What could possibly be better? *Another similar account!* "Obviously," you say. Well, not quite so obvious. Here we have a dividing line: The real pro and the salesperson who's so enamored by recent successes, he/she forgets how it happened and slacks off.

Things change. Now, I'm not suggesting holding onto key accounts is to be taken lightly. I'm the first to attest to the importance, the strategy involved in understanding the personality of a customer. Balancing buyers and hierarchy within a customer's company is itself an art. It's not uncommon for customers to feel lost when the salesperson on whom they depend retires or changes jobs. It's a fact. A salesperson can become so essential to customers that when that person leaves, the customer is uncomfortable with the replacement, opening an avenue for a competitor. (If you're the competitor, you should be ready to take advantage of that situation). When the salesperson who always found a way to make his own people bend; to settle things down after a major rift evolves between his company and the customer; it's when that salesperson takes another job that customers change suppliers. It's that human factor, *stability equals confidence.* Sales management must recognize the intricate part that certain salespeople play in maintaining accounts and offer incentives that keep their key people selling.

Back to the point: Salespeople can't rest on their laurels. Holding onto an account, though essential, takes somewhat less ingenuity than developing one. The amount of effort seeking new accounts shouldn't lessen with success, but ultimately it does. One company I represented decided to offer a commission increase for all new accounts opened during a certain time period. When the offer was made, I invested additional time on their products, which, in turn, produced more sales and RFQ's. He was one of those managers that listen, that recognize incentives come in dollar signs. I'm not sure who thought of that tactic, but it was a major spark for me and my other outside sales employee, and new accounts were the result.

Attention managers! Money, that's what it's about. Try the commission increase yourself, being sure to extend the dates, where a new customer is inevitable because of a salesperson's efforts. Don't ever exclude a salesperson's commission with a technicality; that's tantamount to breaching the ethical line. Manufacturers' agents face that reality every day. I've seen some blatant, even criminal, commission frauds. Restricting a salesperson's commissions doesn't make sense! Nothing is accomplished, everything goes in reverse, and everyone loses.

A company can inadvertently put themselves in a position where their salaried salespeople's commission is jeopardized because of successes. The notion that it's possible to increase sales by downsizing a successful salesperson's area and adding additional salespeople within it, is questionable. If territory changes are made, salespeople in question must be rewarded with higher commission rates as pay back for accounts they developed in a lost territory. Self-starting salespeople aren't to be turned off or they may be off somewhere else. I doubt the validity of that practice. Think about it—you discourage a topnotch moneymaker and add an unknown.

Managers take to heart: *Creativity requires contentment.* You won't stimulate salespeople with titles or backslapping. SHOW THEM THE MONEY.

Salespeople pursue your opportunities! When you tackle large companies anew, those over 1000 employees, especially 3000, or more, you'll need intelligent persistence. Getting to the decision-maker, the decision changer in large corporations is difficult; seemingly an impossible hurdle requiring ongoing determination. It is at such a place, where your assertiveness, and creative juices are needed to acquire inside information. A place where self-confidence and strength in the face of indifferent engineers, one dimensional purchasing people, and department managers with unreasonable product comparisons is a must. A place like many, where unless there is a problem, they're too shorthanded to consider a new device, or maintenance services, even though it improves their product or building. It's a place like this where many outside salespeople walk away. A place you should hit at 4 PM when it's raining, and the parking places are filled. A place like no other to exercise your skills. A place where *once you're in you're in* and everybody knows it. You must believe in yourself to tackle such DPB's and that's what we are striving for.

If you're successful developing a new account, a large one with a promising future, celebrate with dinner. Then get up early the next morning and muse over what to say to other accounts you're soliciting. Later get out your directories and search for other potential customers, don't wait for furnished leads.

A never-ending endeavor to build more business spells more money, but sometimes merely keeps the status quo. One large customer doesn't mean lasting success, nor does 10 or 20. Things go wrong: Bankruptcy; management changes; companies are sold, closed, or moved; a competitor with a better widget comes along; your product fails; their products fail; your decision-maker retires, or the worst of all, an equal product is introduced at a better price. And, that's only a partial list. Therefore, new accounts must be the order of the day.

So get back out there: *Winners never cross the finish line.*

CHAPTER 10

LITTLE THINGS MEAN A LOT

the truth will take you there

The premise of this chapter, being particular with details, may be met with "I know, I know," attitude by longtime salespeople. Little things do make a difference. You have a conversation with a buyer by phone or visit, and a mutual interest is discovered. The buyer likes to fish and you know a place he hasn't tried. Without mentioning it during your conversation, send a brochure on the location with a note. Don't pitch your product with the note, although it would be okay to send the note on a company memo, that's finessing. It's best not to ask about the note or repeat the same exercise. Once is enough, otherwise your efforts may be felt as the arm-around-the-shoulder charade.

The above suggestion works wonders, but keep it in reserve. The following is a must: If you talk to a buyer about an extra specification sheet or something of

mutual interest and promise to send material, you darn
well better do it, even if it was just a passing comment.
I've traveled with salespeople that make comments of
that nature, never intending to follow up. Customers
and DPB's don't always remember what you do, *but
never forget what you don't.* A timely follow-up gives
the buyer or decision maker a sense of your depend-
ability. They have been subconsciously sold. I was 98%
efficient in that area, and it stretched over many years.
I guarantee its effectiveness. Remember my earlier
suggestion? Make notes about follow-up needs and
put it in your top pocket. You'll be reminded, when the
shirt is removed at the end of the day.

Next, we'll look at inference comments. We've talked
about the telephone operator with your company
screwing up work you've done to acquire a new customer
with rude or abrupt handling of a phone inquiry. The
salesperson needs to be equally aware of their own
comments that serve to self-incriminate, it happens
in countless ways.

Let's say the product you're selling comes from
overseas. For most companies imported goods are an
everyday purchase item; however, when you know your
competitor's product is American-made, don't say "the
boat was delayed" or "customs held your shipment."
You've inferred that your product has a potential
delay that the competition doesn't. I had an inside
salesman who excused late deliveries with the "boat
delayed" comment. He insisted all customers knew their
products were made oversees, so why not tell them
the truth about the delay? He didn't want to hear my
reasoning about the competition. You should also know
customers' idiosyncrasies. In another case, the owner
decision-maker in question did have a burn-on against
foreign product, because unfair tariffs were destroying
his export business. Reason finally prevailed, and the
inside contact accepted my position.

It's usually best to keep any outside sourcing such as machining, finish painting, or other operations required for your product, quiet, especially if competition does painting in-house, and you don't. In spite of these facts your attention to detail may seem overbearing to some cohorts. We're back to the shoe salesperson scenario. AGAIN, THE BUYER IS INFLUENCED BY UNCONSCIOUS IMPRESSIONS.

Going that extra step works wonders. You're having a tough time closing a deal or opening an account. The "C" word, "Communication," is the cause. The buyer says, "Yeah we plan to order it, but Neva Ssab, the big cheese, has got to give her approval." You talk to Neva, and she agrees your product needs to be ordered, but would like to go over it again with the buyer. Later they both say they did talk, but didn't remember agreeing on anything. Procrastination can go on forever. Either they're being truthful, and are inefficient, or they're waiting on their present vendor to match your price and holding you off, or both. In any case, the bottom line is—no order.

Arrange another visit with the big cheese, knowing she can interrupt the buyer at will. Suggest there's never a better time than now and ask that she call the buyer at that moment and make a decision. Better still, ask Neva to ask the buyer to join your meeting and with the three of you together, utter the words "I've got no objection... buy it." A meeting arranged like that is one of those little things that mean a lot. Get the order before you leave; it worked for me.

The next example fits here because it concerns extending yourself the extra mile. Upon shipment, your company's product doesn't meet specification. Your company then passes the blame, demonstrating how the drawings from the customer were incorrect. You check, and the customer's engineering department agrees they made an oversight; when this situation occurs the salesperson is up to bat. Though the customer was at fault, avoid even the slimmest flavor of a demeaning response.

Sometimes a purchasing department will blame your company, regardless of where fault lies. Perhaps the customer had internal problems within their communication process; don't allow that to manifest itself by you losing the account. If you try to correct the problem at the purchasing level only, you could get whacked. Check past purchasing, find out who else is getting hit with the reprimand within the customer's company. That's the person who's going to be your problem. In other words, get to where the buck stops. That person needs to be tactfully informed of their own incorrect prints, along with checks your company will initiate to avoid a reoccurrence. Don't ever allow an account to slip away, because you're not willing to step up to the plate. SEEK AND MEND. *You can't be acquitted, if you don't talk directly to the judge.*

If you're concerned how others might respond to your assertiveness and therefore are reluctant to speak, you're stymied before you begin. Follow your truth; don't deny it. The journey will make you stronger and more enlightened.

Being truthful with oneself about all things is laborious. I've experienced communication with those struggling with that difficulty. To realize the ultimate experience in any endeavor, reach for personal truthfulness, regardless of how awkward it feels. You'll sense an epiphany the moment you break through. What a great avenue for the timid to explore, a way to shake your concern about others' opinions. *Personal respect for an individual must be a prerequisite to value their judgment; therefore, strangers don't qualify.* Now, you're free to approach anyone about your products, even stumble in your presentation, and not feel apprehensive. *Why should you?*

Relish this thought; "It's now, this moment, that I'm alive and fulfilled." Imagine that as a consequence of truth. Veracity can deliver us through times when some would put us down, and through times of anguish or pain when we would drown in our own despair. The journey allows us to mature. We've made it to the present, now there is space to grow. The truth is often harsh and revealing but, in itself, makes possible the best that life offers. Many have lived and never comprehended it.

CHAPTER 11

HISTORY TELLS US MONEY IS NOT A MEASURE OF SUCCESS

old salespeople never die; their successes live on

It's time for lamenting: The stuff we sell or their consequence can last many lifetimes. Too often on my car CB radio (yeah, I still use one for expressway traffic advisories), I've heard a trucker complain about four-wheelers screwing things up on the highway. One day I reminded an extra-loud trucker that they'd have nothing to haul if the salespeople in their four-wheelers didn't sell it. He said he wasn't referring to the salespeople, even confiding his wife was a real estate agent.

Whether you're selling to an individual for their own use, or someone who represents a company, your product or products go into service for their lifetime. Many last longer or influence the living experience well beyond our brief span on this planet. Architectural specification sales have left their impact through trails of structures. Skyscrapers, and even pyramids, are creations of the *Human Spirit* that testify to all our philosophical complexities.

When I add sugar to my cereal, it's possible the electric motors I sold to a centrifuge manufacturer, whose machines are used in the sugar cane industry were responsible for its taste. Gears are used to manufacture printing presses. The gears I sold for that application produce labels for foods on grocery store shelves that I buy. Salespeople are intricate throughout the free enterprise system that we all need.

How about the house the trucker's wife sold? What life experiences will happen to the family that bought it? Some person sold a builder on the advantages of certain materials that were selected for use in the Empire State building. Someone sold the concrete to a contractor for the foundations of the high school, where you were educated, and a salesperson convinced an architect which acoustics to specify for the gym. The desk and chair where I sit, the computer I'm using, the book you read, the clothes you wear, and not least of all, the shoes on your feet—a salesperson was there.

I wonder who sold the 1901 Ford I recently saw on display at a shopping center. I wonder who sold its tires to Mr. Ford. I wonder who sold the skylight to the general contractor above the shopping center that gave light for the exhibit.

If you're good in outside sales, you're an irreplaceable asset. There are degrees of talent in all walks of life. We all appreciate the difference in carpentry. I've known mediocre and talented engineers. Unfortunately, if we choose the wrong surgeon, only our survivors are there to know. The point being, the talented, dedicated outside salesperson stands apart. You can't be replaced, and everyone knows it, even if they never say it.

Hey! What happened with the game of five-card stud and the percentage chance of catching an inside straight? Never bet an inside straight on the come, we always hear. Obviously, to have that situation, you must start with three up cards and one down. So, let's return to the poker game. The $44.00 pot has nothing to do with the odds. Of our six players, three besides yourself remain in the game, that's a total of nine more up cards you see besides your own. Two players folded after their first up card, and that's two more cards you saw. Remember, the filling card for your inside straight didn't show up on the table. Therefore, 4+9+2=15 cards removed from the total, where your four elusive filling cards hide. It matters not where they're concealed. Like black holes: what's revealed gives clues to what you can't see. So, 52-15=37, and with four different suits, that's four cards to fill your straight, giving you a 10.8% chance of catching it. After a couple of beers and $44.00 in the pot, who cares? Besides, you could keep raising the last bet and bluff everybody out. Remember the screw-ups by the robots in Chapter one? What boring poker players they would be.

It's often said one must take the sour along with the sweet. As an outside salesman I can attest to lots of both, and, I have chosen to continue the banquet for a long time.

It's so sweet when a large order you thought was lost weeks ago suddenly shows up near the end of the day as an attachment to an e-mail, or on the fax machine; I love when that happens.

It's sour when you know that your products are best-suited for a potential customer, but Horatio, the buyer, begins dating Clementine, your competitor's saleswoman.

It's sweet when you get lucky and hit upon a DPB, just as they begin looking for your type of product.

It's sour when you discover all your written quotes have been used to keep the present vendor's pricing, your competitor, in line. (Suck it up and keep selling.)

It's sweet when you get that paycheck with the first substantial commission included.

It's sour when someone else steps in near the end of closing the big sale and takes credit.

It's sweet when your peers give praise for your success.

It's sour... no more. There's enough sweet to drown out the sour. Hopefully, your "sweet" in outside sales will far outweigh the sour. I believe what you've read here will stimulate your own creative juices. Remember, be yourself, trust yourself, and good things will happen.

Good selling, everyone!

Chapter 12

Part One
On Being A Manufacturers' Agent

sign your life on the dotted line, then jump

Reading Chapter Twelve will provide real-life facts so you can decide if being a manufacturer's agent is for you. You may prefer a secure sales position offering advancement opportunities within a manufacturing, distribution or service company. This chapter will enlighten your decision or at least answer questions about your potential as an independent rep. For those caught in a dead-end job, becoming a manufacturers' agent offers the possibility of finding happiness at the end of the rainbow. The commitment doesn't begin until you've mortgaged your house or closed out your savings account for funds to live and bankroll your venture. A working spouse helps, then again perhaps you have ample cash. In any regard, deposit your inhibitions, now jump.

Although what follows is intended for ICBBS, others, regardless of title, who are involved in outside sales, will appreciate its descriptive nature. Certain parts may seem I'm suggesting that an agent should be wary of some manufacturers, and I am. Unfortunately, it goes both ways, as I point out at the end of the book in the special section for manufacturers seeking agents.

I offer the following proposal to prospective manufacturers' agents and to managers or owners of manufacturing companies who are considering marketing through agents. Are you ready to repeat after me? "Manufacturer, Do You Take This Manufacturers' Agent To Be Your Lawfully Committed Partner?" and, "Manufacturers' Agent Do You Take This Manufacturer to..."

What is a manufacturers' agent? Simply an independent salesperson not employed by anyone, but contracted by several non-competing companies to sell their products or services. Manufacturers' agents sell everything from industrial and commercial items and services to furniture. In my case, as an industrial salesman I've represented several electric motor manufacturers all producing electric motors of different types. I've also represented two companies that manufactured gears, enclosed and open, products closely allied to electric motors.

My example is extremely important. A manufacturers' agent's success depends on representing companies that are closely allied. To better understand the last sentence, consider non-agent competition. Most of the largest manufacturers or distributors using salaried salespeople offer a combination of products. A manufacturers' agent combines several separate companies' products to compete with the variety offered by the large manufacturer or distributor. (Insurance agents do the same thing.) The manufacturer, in a relationship with a manufacturers' agent, is known as the Principal.

Now is the time to mention that a manufacturers' agent receives no salary, no expenses, nothing, in compensation from those they represent, except commission. Then again, there's independence, freedom, personal satisfaction, and the potential of big bucks down the road. But I'm getting ahead of myself. Let's go to the beginning.

We'll commence with a new startup agent. Becoming an independent manufacturers' agent doesn't require a warehouse, stock, employees, or even an office. Use your spare bedroom, or just shove your bed into a corner. Having sales experience helps, but it's not necessary. If you're the sort who likes meeting new people, that's tantamount to success.

Choosing the material to sell is the first step and will depend on your background. Perhaps you work for a company that manufacturers automated widgets. You know that product well and know what customers buy them. You're also aware of other products those same customers must purchase. Manufacturers of those other products become additional opportunities for representation.

Here's how to get those new lines. The quickest way is to check Agency Sales magazine, the voice of MANA (Manufacturers Agents National Association), 16 A Journey Street, Suite 200, Aliso Viejo, CA 92656. Ph 877-626-2776. Their classified ads list companies seeking agents, and their on-line services for members is a good tool. Visit manaonline.org

You may be familiar with Thomas Register and Sweets Directories, both of which once published large volumes of books. The Thomas Register was many volumes, over three feet wide, and listed manufacturers of every conceivable product. Sweets were equally impressive books with building and architectural products. Their directories listed companies by product but both discontinued hard copies and are now available on-line. Thomas Register is now ThomasNet and can be found at thomasnet.com. Sweets Books are now McGraw Hill Construction Sweets Network, and are available at products.construction.com If you still want past dated hard copies, try e-bay or amazon.

There are other on-line ways for finding the type of products or services you want to sell. Your personal computer expertise can guide you through Google and other search engines. Attending trade shows in your realm of interest is an excellent way to establish key contacts. A list of trade show participants offers potential. Search trade show websites for particulars.

Getting companies under contract to sell their products or services takes time. Obviously, getting your first orders takes more. You'll need that large nest egg. Ask yourself if you can live on a zero income for a year or two. Is your spouse willing to assist with a paycheck? Purchasing an existing agency is another way to start. Again, check Agency Sales.

You'll be writing letters to manufacturers to acquire new lines. Letters are most effective, as e-mails are more likely to be ignored or end up in spam, and a fax diminishes the importance of an introductory letter. It's necessary to know which manufacturers use agents and which normally market through their own salaried sales staff. Calling the manufacturer to assure you write to the correct person is best and can sometimes lead to an immediate conversation with key personnel. If you do speak with someone, a letter, e-mail or fax should be sent as a follow-up contact depending on the preference of whom you reached. If a company's product is exactly what you're looking for but already well-marketed, write them anyway, even when you know they use salaried salespeople. If you're known in your field or have impressive credentials and your letter of inquiry is enticing they may make a change to an agent, or who knows, make you an irresistible offer to work for them. Anyway, the exercise of relentlessly pursuing companies to represent will develop your persistence skills, and persistence is a key ingredient for an outside salesperson.

Now comes *The Letter*, the one sent by a new agency to prospective Principals. Yes, you can develop it as a form letter, but often, depending on your widget interest, should be made personal with particular reference to specific details. As I will point out, sales experience is not mandatory to be an agent but in this case we'll assume you have experience in your field in some way. Maybe you were in production, purchasing, outside sales, maybe inside sales. Perhaps you worked in the warehouse or plant. Within your letter use the company you worked for as your primary reference, then factor in the other complimentary products you plan to package as an agent. It's important to reflect on the products of the company you're writing and why they suit your sales plan as a manufacturers' agent. Don't make dollar predictions, even if you're asked; that shouts amateur.

Advise the manufacturer when your agency is a new venture. Indicate the territory you wish to cover. Inform them that you work with an exclusive territory contract only. I'll get more into that later. Maybe you'll mention the name of your ex-employer, maybe not. Perhaps you'll mention your position, maybe not. If you have sales experience, no maybes. Again, whenever possible, call ahead, get names with companies you write and explain the reason for the call. Tell the operator you've seen their product on-line and you're interested in selling it. When you ask the operator if they use manufacturers' agent to market their products, and the operator knows what you're talking about, that's a good sign, so keep talking. Then, if you're connected immediately to the correct person, be brief. Tell that individual you're interested and will send further information. If a conversation develops, get detail and confirm with that person they use agents to sell their materials. If the answer is a positive "no," move on to the next call.

Go for the name of the marketing, sales manager or owner. If you don't have an immediate conversation, you have a name to write. If no one responds to your original letter, a follow-up letter could refer to your first letter as a *proposal that was never answered*; that gets their attention.

Following is a sample of a letter from an individual just starting in the rep business. If you had a conversation with someone about representation before writing them, the letter would have a confirmation introduction and likely refer to a detail you discussed.

Name
Address
City
Phone E-mail Fax

Date

Mr./Mrs. Shirley Ace
Ace Manufacturing Co
100 Main St.
Wonderfulville, HA 10000

Re: Representation as a manufacturers' agent.

Dear (Person whose name you secured when you called) or Sir/
Madam:

For the past 10 years I have been associated with Best
Manufacturing Company. Through that experience (in a few words
explain your job position), I acquired a thorough knowledge of
automated widgets.

The time is right, and I am pursuing my vision to become
a Manufacturers' Agent. I'd like to sell your (in general terms state
what they manufacture). I plan to develop a closely allied product
group that will complement your products. (If you have already
acquired other lines list them).

My territory will consist of The Hawaiian Islands, (That's
me dreaming). (Being nonspecific explain the states or area you
wish to cover including any particular large city, etc. Later, if you
take the next step, you can be more precise about territory).
As a agent, I work only with an exclusive arrangement for my
area. For the purpose of an agreement I prefer using a standard
contract drafted along the same parameters published by the
Manufacturers Agents National Association, however I am open to
other equitable exclusive agreements.

Are you interested? With a positive response I'll provide
further background details. I am anxious to get selling and would
appreciate an early reply.

Sincerely

Obviously, letters sent to potential Principals from an established agent differ. The first and second paragraph should indicate what products you presently represent and how the widgets of the company you're writing complement them. Most importantly, stick to a simplistic, straightforward style.

There will be time for more written and verbal details, as you progress to a contract. Later, you may wish to send the manufacturer your sample contract. Look at your query or conversations as a proposal for a partnership, not employment. Agents normally continue to pursue new manufactures, as they grow or change.

I've known of salespeople who worked for industrial or electrical distributors then became successful manufacturers' agents, whose customers included the very distributors who employed them—a win-win situation.

Send out as many letters as you find applicable Principals. Make your mailing extensive. It could happen that a great job offer results, and you'll have to do a little soul-searching to determine if being an agent is more important. If you send out more than one hundred letters, that's okay. It's a good practice to explore as many manufacturers as possible the first go round.

Part of an agent's agreement commits you, the agent, to non-competing product lines and services. You can't have it both ways. Your goal is to secure companies making different yet complementary products. Occasionally, a part of one line can compete with another. It's compromise time. Overlaps can oftentimes be worked out with the manufacturers in question, but not always. I've been refused a high-profile new line because of product overlap, yet don't fudge, it's necessary to be forthcoming about products you sell.

Now, some important things to consider. "House accounts" are dreaded words. It simply means the manufacturer will not pay commission on sales in the agent's territory to companies indicated within the contract as house accounts. As I developed my business and became more independent, I refused to represent any company that maintained house accounts. To get started, and if the product line is exceptional, it's okay to agree on a house account whereby they become your account after a designated time. A house account can also be arranged so that you get commission after sales within your territory reaches an agreed upon volume. However, I don't advise either. Companies accustomed to working with agents usually don't suggest house accounts. Be sure a potential Principal recognizes you must always get commission for every sale in your territory, no exceptions. An agent in the true sense never writes an invoice. All income is derived from commissions.

Another thing, be sure Principals recognize that you receive copies of all correspondence within your territory. Tell them to read the following special addition to this book on how to utilize agents. If they have doubts about Manufacturer/Agent agreements, that supplement portion of this book will make their part of a successful relationship clear.

Time is everything. Signing with the wrong Principal at the get-go can spell *sure failure* to an agent, and it happens all the time. Imagine a year invested representing a company that cancels or ignores your agreement. Equally, having a product you're not qualified to sell is a big time-waster. You've lost the year and possibly your stake. BE SURE WHEN YOU SIGN, AND, ALWAYS SIGN, NO HANDSHAKES. EVER! I've heard every expression about buddy systems and handshakes. *Those that push for relationships without contracts are the ones to avoid. Take that to the bank.* We'll detail contracts and their repercussion in a moment.

As I said, the initial list of companies you write seeking new lines should be extensive. And, as you establish a niche within your field, the search for new complimentary products should continue; it's a never-ending process. If one potential customer, DPB, has a need for all your products, that's a perfect situation. If you represent six companies and a potential customer has need for only three, you've cut your productive sales time in half. If it's less than three, you're flirting with failure.

This brings us to a sore spot for me. Some agents take on lines, because the Principal has already established customers producing commissions, knowing all the while the product is outside their expertise, or not complementary to their other lines. At best, they plan to make occasional sales calls to existing customers, taking little or no time for new development. These reps create mistrust within the industry, while mistakenly believing they're helping themselves to easy income. They lose time from their other lines, and eventually the Principal they're milking cancels them, and is forever turned off to manufacturers' agents—a loss all around, not to mention it's downright unethical. I detest those agents for what they've done to our industry. If you contact a manufacturer that experienced an unethical agent, their skepticism is warranted. However, stick to you guns about a firm written agreement.

What could be worse than zero income? Answer: Minus zero income. You should expect surviving two years of standard living expenses at zero income and three more below your norm. Then there's the obvious office and travel expenses, creating the minus zero. Make a list, and don't fudge. Be sure you have a good understanding of your forthcoming business expenses. Include all the details like telephone, insurance, gas and so on. I've not presented a step-by-step expense procedure for setting up an office. There are other books providing that information. You must know what you'll need to live on for a year. As a ballpark figure, add fifteen thousand dollars to that. There will be additional cash needs for part time secretarial help as you cut back your 12-and-15-hour days.

Not everyone starts from zero. Perhaps you have bought an agency. Other beginnings include working for a manufacturer that markets through agents, and when a territory opens, you take the plunge; I've seen that happen and it's a good way to start. There are other beginnings with incoming commissions, but for our purpose we'll deal with steps needed, as you begin or grow.

I wish there was a way to make the following more explicit, some word, some comment that could serve to instill in the reader my sense of experience. We'll just have to settle once again for *"pay close attention."*

Acquiring lines (products to sell) takes us again to Contracts and Agreements. They are the most important documents a manufacturers' agent signs and are as permanent as putting your mark in concrete. Agency contracts heads the list of documents with explosive financial consequences. I've walked away from many tempting product lines, whose contracts were obviously one-sided. When you object to a phrase or stipulation within a manufacturer's agreement and it insults the writer, you'll know to close communication, realizing they just tried the confrontation maneuver on you.

Remember, forget companies that suggest the buddy system or say a handshake's always worked for them, and that's in spite of warm fuzzy feelings you have from conversations. Management may change, or the person with whom you initially deal may leave, or get struck by lightning. Then, without a good written agreement your handshake would mean nothing. And yes, there are also those whose intention is to defraud. Sorry, but it's true! A few examples follow.

Lots of other intricacies are involved in the rep contract. TIME, TIME, TIME—your success or failure depends upon it. It takes so many sales hours to earn $1000 in commissions. If you keep dividing that amount by a growing number of hours, it can reach broke. If this doesn't convince you to follow my guidelines for contracts, then you're one of those people who set themselves up to be knocked off. Why waste your time? Give your stake money to a worthy charity and get a good sales job.

Some of my experiences early on were very costly. Yet like most things, once burned, I learned. Then, because my wife began her rep business years later, I was once again involved in building new lines and interestingly, saw my early behavior reenacted. My wife and I had some of our more spirited (I admit that word is a bit stretched) conversations concerning the signing of agreements during the startup phase of her business.

Problems develop through varied circumstances. New manufacturers' agents need lines. They don't feel beggars can be chooses and are willing to sign a weak agreement or work with no agreement at all. Leave the hand-prints in concrete to movie stars and get the signature.

MANA has a contract you can consider. Read it carefully. If the manufacturer has their own, check it out, then use the MANA contract as a guideline. Joining MANA is conducive to success. Through the years I developed my own simple, sample contract, hoping to avoid intimidating tentative manufacturers whose products I really liked. My sample's part MANA, part ideas taken from other manufacturers contracts I've signed, along with stipulations I wanted to include. My sample contract follows after Part Two of this chapter, however I don't advocate using it, unless your attorney confirms that it's legally binding. If you create your own contract, do your best to keep it simple, as the simple approach is usually more acceptable to manufacturers new to agents. As I said before, depending on conversation with the potential Principal, send them your sample contract before you progress to a final agreement. It serves as a good basic step.

For my part, here are some key words and phrases to watch for in agreements: In the cancellation clause ask for the word GOOD within the sentence, "either party has the right to cancel the contract with GOOD cause." Short of that simply WITH or FOR cause can be considered. Don't accept the sentence "either party may cancel the contract WITHOUT cause." Also, WITHOUT can't be added to WITH to create WITH OR WITHOUT CAUSE. Simply stating "either party may cancel the contract" is not sufficient either.

The language of the cancellation clause must include a 30-day notice. 30 days being the minimum: I always ask for 60 days, with 90 days being the first choice. Most important, a contract must include the sentence, *"If termination occurs, commissions will be paid on all orders received and accepted by the manufacturer prior to the termination date, regardless when shipment is made or invoices rendered."* Don't accept a time-limit payment on commissions for orders in house at termination. If the company you plan to represent refuses, back off, unless there's a reason specific to the type of product involved. There can also be wording within a contract for commission credit on pending quotes at termination. This situation most often occurs with agents in the building products field. As part of the agreement the agent has the right to register quotes at termination. A time limit for an order to follow, say one year, is usually stipulated.

There are variations on when and how commissions are paid, but receiving payment on the tenth of the month following the customer paying the Principal's invoice is most common.

One would normally think exclusivity is implied when a company chooses to sign on manufacturer's agents; not true. Be sure your written agreement is clear about exclusivity. An area or territory is most often defined by state or county boundaries. Some use Zip Codes. It may surprise you how often a manufacturer, unfamiliar with the independent agent concept, will offer their line without an exclusive commitment. Sometimes, if an agent insists on an exclusive contract, it uncovers manufacturers that have several agents crossing territories. The Principal may wing it as long as possible but when it's clear the agent is expecting an exclusive territory some manufacturers may back away; that's exactly what you want.

The next statement is the backbone of an independent representative's agreement. *Whenever a sale occurs within your area, you get credit, get commission for the sale. It doesn't matter if you worked for years to land the account or have never visited the customer, or for that matter didn't even know they existed. If a customer is in your contracted area, you get commission on all sales.* If the Principal you're considering balks at that reality, forget them. Don't lose time. What would you prefer, not having a line you need, or not having a line you need after you're faced with irreconcilable differences and the manufacturer cancels you, or you cancel them? Changing lines after presenting a company's products to customers and DPBs does more than cost time. Now the company you briefly represented is a competitor, and you have given them a foot up and lost credibility with those companies you approached with their product. Get it right the first time. Be sure of the contract. I wish I could somehow make that mandatory, before agents sign on the dotted line.

If you're interested in representing a manufacturer that has not used agents, tread lightly. They may have a difficult time understanding the concept that a Manufacturers' Agent is paid commission for every invoice into the territory, whether or not the agent made the sale. If you're arguing each time commissions are due on orders the agent didn't solicit, it's inevitable you're headed for trouble.

Manufacturers new to agents are notorious for changing their minds about the independent rep concept after they sign agents; that happened to my wife. Some manufacturers may test the waters for a new widget's sales potential, then decide not to stay with it and cancel all agents within months. Unfortunately, I can't offer a hard and fast rule to avoid that circumstance. You've got to smoke out that possibility. Are they using agents for the first time? Is this a new product somewhat unrelated to their present offerings? If the answer to both are yes, dig deeper.

If, for no fault of your own, you're terminated soon after signing an acceptable contract and commissions haven't reached a point where a lawsuit is justified, you're out of luck. Late in my career, I adopted the policy of not representing companies that didn't have at least two years marketing experience through agents. I'm not suggesting you strictly follow that action, but be prepared for misconceptions. Intuition comes into play in this situation.

You may be presented with another approach, one to reject; named accounts. (Briefly defined, you must report to the manufacturer every company you contact). An agreement with that premise becomes so entangled with confusion, misunderstandings, and outright chiseling, it's soon over. But again not before a huge loss of time and credibility. It should be apparent that named accounts as a basis of an agreement would be impossible to monitor. They could receive an order directly from someone you've visited, but don't remember you saying you did. Also, if you send a list of every company you contact, they have a free list of potentials in your territory when they cancel you. Here's the key to success: An agent must have a free hand to make sales visits, sales phone calls, distribute literature, develop a website, exhibit products in local trade shows, and not have concerns about receiving commissions if their efforts result in the customer contacting the manufacturer directly. Often, depending on what you sell, direct contact from customers and DPB's to your manufacturer is the norm.

It's always best to have the same geographical area for all lines. However, in special situations (it happened with me), you may want to cross over your geographical border into an area where your Principal has no agent. This situation occurs when a company is your current customer for one line and they have a need for another product you represent, but you don't have that line in that customer's area. You'll be okay in that situation, as long as you're successfully selling that manufacturer's products to other customers in your regular contracted area. Another similar circumstance isn't okay. Don't rep a manufacturer for one named customer, when you don't have that manufacturer in any of your contracted areas. If you have only one customer on a named account basis for one manufacturer, you're headed for problems. It's best to contract manufacturers for all the same areas to *sustain an equal balance in Principal/Agent relationships.*

For those of you who believe I'm overly pessimistic, you've got it right. Ask yourself this question: "Where will I be in two years, if I haven't established lasting good lines?"

Even long-term problems can occur. First example: I was the first agent a new owner put on after buying his company. After 10 years of success, a personal relationship that included family visits, and my assistance giving his engineer sales experience, he decided I was making too much money. (Money has a strange effect on people). He established a new commission schedule that cut one large account commissions by 75% and all other accounts by 50%. Having a good contract, I contacted a lawyer and began a lawsuit. Eventually, he apologized, my commissions were reestablished, and I continued as his agent. Our relationship was frayed from the experience, but I accepted his apology (it was good business) and eventually reestablished a subdued workable relationship, mostly with the sales manager. Without that contract, it would've been all over.

Another Principal, whom I represented for some time with good success, canceled me outright, when they realized that one customer whom I established with years of prodding, would soon increase volume dramatically. That customer purchased a larger competitor and expected orders to multiply nine or ten times. Adjustments in my Principal's manufacturing facility would be necessary to keep up with their needs. I arranged a meeting with their marketing/engineering manager and my production manager to implement a manufacturing and delivery schedule to accommodate the new expected growing volume requirements. Four days after that visit I received a fax advising that I was canceled immediately. (Can you believe it?) They made the mistake of breaching our contract by not honoring a 30-day cancellation clause. I doubt if they even checked the agreement; in retrospect it likely meant nothing to them anyway. *Again, with a good agreement, I got a lawyer.* This time I accepted a cash settlement on the Saturday before our Monday scheduled trial. What a stupid thing for them to cancel me! The customer's busiest management were called for depositions and hated being involved. Without my inside relationships and guidance that customer's sales were in shambles within two years; they located another supplier. Everyone, except me, lost immediately, and I lost long-term. Just recalling this event distresses me.

Those experiences were unfortunate but true, and I would be remiss if I didn't relate them. It's likely volumes could be written about such experiences. I've made this point before, I'm afraid in many situations, that *"the line for ethical business behavior has been erased and replaced by one that defines criminal behavior."*

The following example crossed all lines and caught me unaware—a blatant criminal experience.

I still recall my attorney's reaction to the story: "He put one over on you" a callous, yet realistic lawyer's interpretation of an unethical self-serving cheat. The company was a Principal with whom my wife signed. After one year a fire destroyed their buildings, and a new corporation was formed. (I had serious doubts about the nature of that fire). A new contract was sent to replace the first. (It likely went to all their reps if they had any). During the first year new customers had been created, and commissions were beginning to show promise.

Then the hitch occurred. I noted a word within a clause of the replacement agreement that in essence said "It's not necessary to pay commission, if that's our choice." No kidding. The wording wasn't that explicit, but was a ambiguous legal phrase with the same result. I objected, and the owner agreed to change it. "Just an oversight," he exclaimed.

There were months of delay getting the contract corrected. During that time my wife enthusiastically pursued DPBs and created orders. The contracts finally arrived with the single word deleted that previously made it useless. However, he hadn't signed either of two copies. The normal procedure is to have the Principal sign two copies of an approved agreement and mail both for the agent to sign. Then the agent returns one copy to the Principal with both signatures. "No problem," I said. "I'll sign both and send them back to you. You sign one and send it back to me." He did so immediately and I filed it away.

You can't guess what happened. After a time and sales later commissions weren't being paid. It progressed to the point where we threatened to sue for our money, but he did not budge, insisting he owed us nothing. Lo and behold, he was right! Satisfied with his signature on the dotted line, when my copy of the contract was returned, I hadn't reexamined the entire document, assuming it was the same as the ones I'd mailed. Only then did I realized, the second page of three pages had been removed—we didn't initialed each page—and replaced with another page that contained the original wording, making the contract useless. He had intentionally not signed the agreements when he mailed them, and I unsuspectedly returned both copies with my signature. I, who considered myself very cautious with contracts, had been duped. We lost $9,500, in commissions, a sum too small to bring suit. Most exasperating was the investment in time.

After presenting that last encounter, I need to wipe away the stigma it leaves, so I want to add, right now: I've had the pleasure of knowing many ethical individuals with manufacturing companies whom I trusted implicitly, and am sure most agents concur.

You might hear, "We'll pay you a finder's fee for customers you bring us." That's totally unacceptable, and anyone that proposes that option knows nothing about manufacturer and agent relationships and should be avoided. A manufacturers' agent's business expenses are similar to those of lawyers or doctors. Regardless of agency size, like a law firm, the manufacturing company contracting with a manufacturers' agent pays for the ongoing practice of the agency: The education; experience; expertise; cost of getting from there to here; time used to create and maintain contacts with countless DPB's, and customers, plus research to find new ones are all big expenses. In short, agents have expense just to be in operation, and that's why any ongoing commissions become payable after signing the contract. To pay overhead, a surgeon's charges include liability of their entire office, plus out-of-pocket expenses, not just the time involved to repair the rotator cuff. In fact, I advocate that neither agent nor manufacturer should enter into a commission contract unless they accept the underlying concepts in this book.

This brings me to another phenomenon of the Principal/Agent relationship. Again, I'll explain through example. I had a customer that manufactured ice-making machinery that they marketed through manufacturers agents. I'm not sure why the engineering manager confided in me, maybe it was because of the long Friday lunches he sometimes suggested. Their unwritten policy was to terminate an independent rep, when their territory produced commissions that exceeded the salary and expenses of hiring a company salesperson. What a shortsighted, ridiculous attitude! Eventually I expressed my dismay at their policy and my business with them suffered.

I've heard of manufacturing companies closing their doors, after canceling manufacturers agents en masse and replacing them with salaried salespeople. An English company I represented canceled all agents, then, within three years, went out of business in the U.S.. It was a bonanza for me. When I was canceled, I got lucky and signed with a different English company, a competitor with better products and management. That happens.

Most companies using agents offer fair agreements. Stay with them. **Don't deviate**. However, if you've decided to go forward with an manufacturer's agreement, and parts of it are a bit confusing, have it checked by an attorney; that would be worth the legal fee.

I've seen some of the most one-sided agreements imaginable. I never understood why someone would bothered presenting them for consideration. The only conclusion was that other reps signed them. **Please,** give yourself a chance to spread your wings as an independent agent. You'll never realize your potential, if you sign your chance away.

To the presidents, sales managers, and owners who abhor the practices depicted in these last pages and resent the implication that manufacturers can't be trusted, that's good. I know you're out there. I appreciate your astonishment. After all, as I said earlier, I've represented many manufacturers with admirable people, whom I'll always hold in esteem.

Chapter 12

Part Two
On Being A Manufacturers' Agent

creativity is a visionary's passion... the good stuff

Yes, being an independent agent offers monetary growth potential not available anywhere else in the sales profession. Time, the single most important word in our lives, is yours. Starve or feast, be rich or poor, or somewhere in between, it's your decision. Even during the struggling years agents can take personal time, when it suits them best—Mondays on the golf course, and Sundays in the office preparing a new visit list.

You're the boss. All your decisions are final. I liked that perk, even during my single years without a better half to share the ups and downs. Today, it's different. Many decisions are reached during discussions in the bedroom. Deductible space? I'll need to ask my accountant about that.

Design your own sales reports. I've written up every sales visit and most phone calls. They're not legible to others, but they serve me well. Establish your own pattern, but follow the fundamentals in Chapter Four. It's never necessary to send a Principal sales reports. I did send customer reports about extensive meetings or strategies to be sure my Principal and I were on the same page. Often, after visiting a DPB following a significant quote, I send reports to my manufacturer. Being cooperative is a must to maintain successful relationships, and giving them feedback on quotes is good business. If you do your job, you'll seldom get pressure from the companies you represent.

Companies sign independent agents for their established presence in the marketplace or to make an inexpensive entry into a market. They also know a new agent will work hard to move product. If you're new, you'll need to work 25 hours a day to convince them you're the correct choice.

Companies recognize that they vie for your time, like having multiple wives or husbands; that's what the relationship implies. However, some Principals seem to believe they're the only company you represent, be ready for that. You'll need to keep Principals cognizant of reality, and remind them your livelihood depends on making them a success. Adopt the following principal as a basis for maintaining independence: ***"It's not we it's you and me."***

The most exasperating set of circumstances between Agent and Principal goes both ways, and it's worth repeating. First, the agent. Some agents acquire new lines, knowing the product is not a good mix with their other efforts, but want the product for the established commissions. They've created an obstacle that continues to hamper Principal/Agent relationships. The manufacturer must confront those agents.

Manufacturers that adopt new unreasonable demands on agents, encourage them to invest little time in developing business for the manufacturer. The agent believes they're justified, because the company changed procedures' from the prescribed agreement. Additionally, when manufacturers don't pay commissions on time or who are unfair with split commissions items, also initiate a "don't work just collect," posture with agents; a poisonous situation leading to divorce. Agents can stay clear of that possibility. Communicate, get past the barrier and consciously question your Principal about negative intuitive feelings.

The Principal/Agent marriage is money-based, its the only purpose for tying the knot. To achieve success, it's critical both parties are honorable and both have long-term intentions.

Here we must insert a disconcerting question, one a Principal may some day ask. Our profit margin is low on this quote: WILL YOU AGREE TO TAKE LESS COMMISSION? Don't! If it's done once, asking with each large quotation will become the norm. Everyone overlooks a simple fact: If your commission is 10% and you're asked to accept 5%, that's not a 5% decrease; IT'S 50% LESS. A 2% cut with a 10% base is 20%. Your time doesn't cost the Principal. When you get the sale in your area, you get the commission. I admit, in one very rare circumstance, because of the potential of a new customer, I made an exception. If a format of reduced commissions is agreed to at contract time (prenuptial), that's O.K.

Children have a knack detecting charisma that exists between themselves and others, young or old. "Complex business relationships are no place for children," one might argue, but the opposite can be true. Great artists through the centuries created from the child within. Imagination is the child's delight, and it's that part of us that senses the potential of things. It's there when

Principal and Agent come together, and you sense a positive future. Regardless, get the contract!

Again, I advocate that neither agent nor manufacturer should enter into a commission contract, unless they accept the underlying concepts in this book. If either is tentative, it's likely things won't work out. I suggest agents read the supplement, *Take A Manufacturers' Agent To Market* to understand the effort manufacturers undertake to find and evaluate you.

If you're convinced being a Manufacturers' Agent holds promise for your breakout, then get involved. It's not always necessary to leave a secure, yet boring, job you tolerate each day to start your company. The details of setting up the office, and most importantly, making calls and sending out letters to secure lines, can come first. Weekends, nights, or days off will be adequate.

This point should be clear: Being a Manufacturers' Agent forces you into an adventurous career. I'm dead serious, no exaggeration. Your mind, will, body and emotional well-being will be tested daily. You're on your own; there is no regiment.

What about rewards? Yes, at last we come to the rewards. Money, income well above average, but wait— lots of prosaic people make money. There's more. Freedom to do your own thing, set your own schedule, meet new people, and for me, the enjoyment of being outdoors.

Creativity, a visionary's passion, becomes your tool, your momentum, that stays the course through good and bad and keeps us all mysteriously working on. Self-confidence swells the character, followed by an ever-increasing sense of satisfaction. You truly reap what you sow. And, when you land that big one, the sale you've worked on for so long, there is a high, a certain charge, a rush of satisfaction that comes only to an outside salesperson, save maybe a skydiver.

Hmmm—mm, I wonder what that feels like?

Agency/Principal Agreement

This agreement is made on the date shown below by and between.

Date:_____

_____("Principal"),

and _____("Agent")

1. Exclusive Representative. Principal grants to Agent the exclusive right (to the exclusion of Principal and all claiming under or through Principal), by acting as Principal's sales representative, to solicit orders for the Principal's goods, equipment and/or services ___**(See exhibit A)**___(Products) within the following geographical or otherwise defined area. ___**(See exhibit B)**___ ___(Territory). Agent agrees not to represent another manufacturer within the defined area whose product or service is directly competitive to Principal.

2. Sales Policy. The prices, and terms of sale (Sales Policies) shall be established by Principal. If possible, notice of Sales Policy changes shall be given by Principal to Agency 30 days prior to changes.

3. Orders and Collections. Orders for Products within the Agent's territory shall be subject to acceptance by Principal. The Principal agrees to refer and/or copy agent on all inquiries, and promptly furnish Agent with copies of all correspondence and pertinent documents between Principal and Customer. All invoices shall be rendered by Principal to Customer , with copies to Agent. Responsibility for collection rests with Principal,; however, Agent agrees to assist Principal with collection when appropriate.

4. Agent's commission. The commission payable to Agent on orders from the Agent's territory shall be deemed earned by agent upon acceptance or delivery of an order by Principal, whichever occurs first. Commission rates shall be ____**(See exhibit C)**____ (Commission Rate). Commission shall be computed on the net amount of the invoice exclusive of freight costs. A Split Commission percentage for a specification originating from one Agent's territory for shipment into another Agent's territory

will be determined as given in _____**(See exhibit D)**_____
(Commission Split). Full commission is paid to Specification Agent
(with information furnished by agent) when shipment is made into
a territory without another Agent. All commissions due agent for
sales in Agent's territory shall be paid on the 10th of the month,
immediately following Principal's receipt of payment from the
customer.

5. Relationship Created. Agent is not an employee of Principal,
but is an independent contractor, who shall have sole control of
the manner and means of performing under this agreement. All
expenses incurred by Agent by promoting Principal's goods
and/or services in connection with this agreement shall be borne
wholly and completely by Agent. Agent does not have any right,
power or authority to create any contract or obligation, either
expressed or implied on behalf of Principal.

6. Term. This agreement is for an initial period of 18 months and
shall automatically renew for successive 1-year periods. Following
the 18-month period, either party may terminate this agreement for
good cause by giving written notice via certified mail to the other.
The "Termination Date" shall become effective 90 days after
notice is given. If the agreement is terminated, all orders received
and accepted by Principal from Agent's territory prior to effective
date of termination will be due commission as given in Paragraph
Four regardless of when orders are shipped or invoices rendered.
Agent shall be entitled to receive full commission from quoted
projects that become orders within one year following effective
date of termination.

7. Hold Harmless. Principal shall save Agent harmless from and
against and indemnify Agent for all liability, loss, costs, expenses or
damages howsoever caused by reason of any product (whether or
not defective), or any act or omission of Principal, including but not
limited to any injury (whether to body or property) sustained by
any person or to property, and for infringement of any patent rights,
or third parties, and for any violation of municipal state or federal
laws or regulations governing their products or their sale. Agent
shall hold Principal Harmless from and against and indemnify
Principal from any loss, costs, expenses or damages incurred by
Agent fulfilling this agreement.

8. Notices. This agreement contains the full and final agreements between the parties, and becomes effective when signed by parties noted hereon. Any notice demand or request shall be in writing and deemed effective twenty-four hours after having been deposited in the United States mail, postage prepaid, registered or certified to the addressee at their main office. Any party may change their office address for purposes of this agreement by written notice in accordance herewith.

(Principal): _____

By: _____

Signature: _____

Date: _____

Principal's Address: _____

_____

(Agent): _____

By: _____

Signature: _____

Date: _____

Agent's Address: _____

_____

EXHIBIT A - PRODUCTS

EXHIBIT B - TERRITORY

EXHIBIT C - COMMISSION

EXHIBIT D - COMMISSION SPLIT

This sample is provided by Walter Nussbaum as a guideline and is not intended for legal use.

SUPPLEMENT

TAKE A MANUFACTURERS' AGENT TO MARKET

SUPPLEMENT

TAKE A MANUFACTURERS' AGENT TO MARKET

then have your cake and eat it too

Note: This is a STAND-ALONE SUPPLEMENT to this book. An earlier edition of Take A Manufacturers' Agent To Market was printed as a booklet. The following version is updated and edited, yet remains a stand-alone publication. Therefore, parts of the following have unavoidable similarities to Chapter Twelve, from Secrets From The Street, written for agents. Acronyms are defined on page 216.

This 6,500 word volume presents a surefire system, whereby manufacturers can effectively market their products through Manufacturers' Agents. It offers candid, how-to detail to engage, and sell product through a network of agents. It guides manufacturers to agents they need while avoiding hidden pitfalls. For those already utilizing manufacturers' agents, *Take A Manufacturers' Agent To Market* contains everything you don't already know.

First, I'll define "manufacturers' agent" for those unfamiliar with the term. Simply stated, a manufacturers' agent is an independent salesperson, not employed, but contracted by a selective number of manufacturing companies, whose products are complementary, not competitive. The agent's income is totally derived from sales commissions calculated from a specified exclusive territory. Other than normal backup, providing literature, bookkeeping, engineering, quotations, and effective communication, the manufacturer has no outside sales expense—zero, zip. A manufacturer that forms this partnership with an agent is known as the *Principal.*

Is it actually feasible for a manufacturer to increase sales volume and lower expenses without paying a single salaried outside salesperson? Definitely! How? Utilize manufacturers' agents, salespeople who are totally self-motivated.

Manufacturers' agencies vary in size from a one-person operation to twenty or more. A firm of one, two or three outside salespeople is common. Products vary widely: From chemicals, screw machine parts, or material handling equipment to specialty ceilings or building materials. An agent's customers cover the gamut too: manufacturer, distributor, OEM, (original equipment manufacturer) architect, contractor, user, or peripheral outlet. I sold electric motors and gears, two closely allied products, into the OEM market. *Closely allied* is a key issue we'll explore.

Manufacturers that plan to market through a network of manufacturers' agents should be aware of potentially hazardous side effects. Vital information needed by the manufacturer to select agents is often elusive. The insight in these pages will clarify agent/manufacturer relationships and reveal subtle agency nuances that foster success.

If you're already using manufactures' agents, everything you don't already know is here, too. I'll explore fundamentals that optimize an agent's impact and bridge the gap from mediocrity to success. You'll learn to interpret agents' motives, then guide and adapt each agent to your specific area of sales and manufacturing. Perhaps you're open to the concept of manufacturers' agents, but are concerned you'll lose control or accountability of outside sales. What's explored here will convince you that agents don't need strings, thus freeing your precious time.

Manufacturers' Agents are a perfect fit for many companies.

1. Small, privately financed companies that can't afford salaried outside salespeople can grow rapidly with independent manufacturers' agents.

2. Mid-sized manufacturers whose products or services require technical sales have a natural affinity with manufacturers' agents, given the agent's inherent expertise and broad perspective handling complementary lines.

3. Manufacturers' Agents are a perfect fit for overseas manufacturers with US offices and/or warehousing/manufacturing.

4. Large global manufacturers appoint manufacturers' agents when sales lag in certain pockets of their products. A manufacturer of large AC (Alternating Current) electric motors that also produces a line of small universal motor would belong in this category. Their outside salaried salespeople, accustomed to particulars required for selling large AC electric motors, would have only marginal penetration with users of small universal motors. On the other hand, manufacturers' agents selling several lines of small motors

would have sales contacts in the proper niche and be better-suited to sell universal motors. I recall an international company that manufactured AC and DC (Direct Current) motors and used reps for DC electric motor sales. Its better for Global companies to use agents for their specialties rather than salaried people who can't get the job done. Get it? "The Best Of The Better," go ahead have that piece of cake.

Don't Break The Law, Play It Fairway

keep an even keel, sail into the sunset

To help avoid misunderstandings or legal problems down the road, let's start with parameters.

Engaging a manufacturers' agent is, in essence, contracting their time without pay, especially when an agent accepts a product in a territory without existing sales. Agents gamble, investing tens of thousands of dollars of time during the developmental stage in a territory before realizing a profit. They're in it for the long-term payoff. So, when you consider using agents, remember that reps are in the business for *big* future profits; that's the attitude you want. Eventually an agent's commissions may become greater than the overhead cost of a salaried salesperson in the same territory. Play it fair, don't entertain the notion of replacing reps, once their commissions exceed a company salesperson's salary.

Even with an "ethics be damned" attitude the bottom line is best served by staying the course. Why? The outside salesperson you hire will likely be inexperienced, and sales will sink. The agent will likely contract for a competing line. With intimate knowledge of your products and established relationships with the existing customers, that agent will sail away with your business. I knew of two cases where canceled agents began manufacturing competitive product themselves. Furthermore, once you've canceled agents, the word gets out, and you're unable to contract with them again. It's like declaring bankruptcy, no one will take a chance with you. Keep in mind: The more the rep sells, the more you profit. If your hand cramps signing huge commission checks, massage it. With manufacturers' agents you truly reap what you sow. *Trust is a must!* I'm talking about the real thing, *credibility*, not a ploy to manipulate the agent's thinking.

A true story: A manufacturer called regarding my consulting service that instructs the proper approach for setting up a network of manufacturers' agents. Prior to making an appointment, he asked a few questions and became perplexed with some of my replies. Here is how I remember that exchange: "You mean," he said, exasperated from my interpretation of a sales issue, "I can't engage more than one agent in a territory? If that's the case," he went on to say "I'll expect them to represent only my product."

"Can't be done that way," I answered. "One agency to a territory is basic. Agents gamble considerable time, without profitable return. That's part of the process. Without exclusivity there's no incentive for an agent to develop interest in your product or service. Others who you appoint later in the same area could merely cut their commissions to be more competitive. With no investment in time why wouldn't they? Additionally, agents offer complementary products that enhance sales for your company. That's part of the rationale for hiring a manufacturers' agent."

"Unacceptable," he countered his tone becoming sullen. "To give a protected area, I want exclusivity in return."

"Well, if you believe your product could stand alone and support a salesperson in a territory, you may want to consider a salaried outside salesperson. With a yearly salary, plus bonus, benefits, and expenses, you'll have exclusivity. You'll also be the one gambling two or three years of cash to get your product going, cash that may never be recouped. Your investment would depend on your new employees' talents and how long they stick around." His next response told me the conversation was over.

If, as a manufacturer, you're dubious about these requirements and find them awkward or unsettling, here's an analogy that may take the pain away, especially if you play golf.

Consider a longtime golfer that hasn't lowered his score in years in spite of long hours at the driving range. In desperation he decides to take lessons from his club's pro. The professional works with his new student, first changing his stance and grip, then concentrating on his swing to improve his follow-through.

The old golfer's next 18 holes are a disaster. "This feels awkward as hell, it can't be right," he complains to his friends while reaching for his wallet after the match.

"I played terrible," he declares when he returns for his next lesson, "I felt all out of sync. I had one of the worst rounds I've shot in years."

"Sure," the pro answered. "You're learning new ways, and even though it's the *CORRECT* approach, *adjusting to change takes time,* but, if you stick with what I'm teaching you, stay with it, I guarantee you'll improve dramatically and likely knock 10 strokes or more off your score. *The old way (thinking) became habit and limited your potential.*"

"Show me that stance again," the old golfer said, grabbing his club.

FINDING AND SELECTING MANUFACTURERS' AGENTS

hide and seek

Considering the vast array of manufactured items, the process of selecting agents required for specific products is arduous. Where are the agents? Agency Sales Magazine, published by MANA (Manufacturers Agents National Association), offers classified ads for Principals and agents. MANA also has an excellent website search for members and associate members (manaonline.org). Some national journals have "Agent Wanted" classified sections. Trade magazines are excellent publications for placing ads. Attending trade shows is a good way to find agents. If you exhibit, put a small sign on your booth, "Interested in Manufacturers' Agents." Your company will likely receive periodic letters from agents asking about representation. Instruct your staff to recognize them, ensuring the letters are properly routed. Be sure your operator or phone system are in-tune for inquiries from agents.

Selecting the best agents from the get-go is a must for building your agent sales organization. *Early bad choices can literally put you out of business.* A startup agent in a territory usually requires a year, maybe two or three, to develop sales; that's especially true, if your product is also new. It's like the blind spot in your car's rear view mirror, don't take the hit, turn your head, look carefully before you pull out. Here's how. *Check the companies the prospective agent represents before you commit and be sure that their products complement one another and likewise what you manufacture.* Never, never appoint an agent whose lines are far removed. Ideally, but not likely, if a one-person agent has six lines, the customers or DPBs (Definite Possibility of Business) they're soliciting should have potential to use all six. If your widget's are compatible with less than three of their other lines, there must be extenuating circumstances or pass on that agency.

Effective selling time is the key. Simple logic will tell you the efficiency sales/time rate of selling unrelated products. I can't think of a legitimate excuse or explanation why an established agent should take on your line when it's not complementary to any of their other products. None! If they do, you have an agent whose only interest is taking fallout commissions without working to expand or maintain sales, a deadly deed. I call them *easy money* reps. They're unethical and, worse, give our profession a bad name. You'll hear more about *"easy money" reps*, as we continue. On the other hand, a rep handling complementary lines increases your sales potential. Every sales visit that agent makes is a potential customer for your widget. Sales leads furnished by one manufacturer can result in sales for another.

If the agency you're considering is the multi-rep type, you're likely to find they have diverse groups of products. For the purpose of this book, I consider agencies with more than three outside salespeople multi-rep agencies. That's good as long as the complementary hypothesis is applied. Specifically, one rep or faction within the multi-rep company should be assigned to a group of similar products.

When you utilize multi-rep agencies, the interviews that precede the relationship normally consist of management meeting management. That's great, as it's important that you be on the same page. More significant is the particular rep, or reps, who'll sell your product. Insist on spending time with those particular persons. That's likely the agency's procedure, you shouldn't have to ask. Be sure the agency compensates their outside salespeople with commission, as that's the basis for using agents. Always make your selection based on the outside salesperson. Though an owner agent should have the wherewithal to hire aggressive outside people, you need to be sure.

Today, some agencies require upfront advances from manufacturers who have no presence in a territory. You'll find this most often with large rep firms who's reputation commands it.

Sub-reps (agents having an agreement with another agent to handle part of an area that the primary agent doesn't cover) are definitely not recommended. From my experience I've learned that efficiency is reduced by 90% or more. Reps using sub-reps have a probability of being the "easy money" types.

It's my opinion that agency owners who remain in the field are the most potent reps. Agencies with one, two, or three outside salespeople fall into this category. They are the most committed, and each individual salesperson has staying power that assures years of operation.

Ask the agents you're considering if they are willing to explain their method of locating decision-makers within the DPB's they contact. This strategy assures they'll develop new business for you, not just romance existing customers.

In any business customers are lost for reasons beyond control, it's inevitable. I contend that the task of establishing new accounts is more important than maintaining existing ones. *The better salespeople maintain existing accounts.* The best open new ones. "The best of the better", you should sense that attitude in your agent.

Now for the exceptions. There's always an exception. It could happen that a new rep, still fashioning a group of products, could unknowingly take on unrelated widgets, some far-removed from yours; that's possible with new agents, they're feeling their way. Scrutinize them closely, but cut new agents some slack. New, one-person agencies are an exciting avenue for utilizing independent agents. We all know the early bird gets the worm, and new reps are raring to go, they need the money. You may prefer waiting until you determine that a new agent has developed a good product grouping, has direction, and seems to be in it for the long term. It's sort of like a single person meeting the newly divorced person just released into the dating world. Best to give them a little time to learn the score, before you get involved. However, don't take the last sentence as a hard, fast rule.

For the rep who's just getting started, previous outside sales experience is a consideration. Check the rep's resume. Outside sales savvy, especially familiarity with your product, is a big plus. With new reps you're *not* looking for someone with management skills. You want the person with charisma, fortitude, and street smarts. It's tough out there and someone with experience taking the knocks salespeople encounter each day has an advantage. The agent's management ability comes, as business grows.

I'm not suggesting you dismiss startup reps without prior sales experience. If they worked in production, the parts department, purchasing, or other areas that exposed them to widgets similar to your product, give them a good look. They may be the hungriest of all— diamonds in the rough. I knew a PA (purchasing agent) who was super, and success followed. Talk to them more than once, then allow your intuition to provide the answer. If they read my book, Secrets From The Street, that's a big plus.

Included is an example of a letter as a guideline for manufacturers initiating contact with a manufacturers' agent.

Letter to Prospective Manufacturers' Agents

Date
Dear Mr./Mrs.
Company, address, etc.

An important fact for today: If our products are compatible, adding them to your existing lines can significantly improve your agency's sales commissions.

We have seen your ad/listing in MANA, (or It was nice meeting you at the _____trade show, or Thanks for inquiring about/ etc.)

We are manufacturers of_____. Would the advantages and unique qualities of our_____ be a good mix with the products you presently sell or plan to sell?

Our company is...(give company ownership, history, year started, number of employees, etc.).

We've enclosed literature so you may determine if our products, and company profile fit your sales history and direction. Check our website at... If you are interested, please provide a list of your present principals, (and) territory interest, (and salespeople in the field). *The words in parenthesis may vary or be excluded, depending upon what you already know about their size.*

We understand that there is an ethical commitment between manufacturers' agents and manufacturers. We are prepared to enter into an exclusive written agreement and will be happy to send a sample contract when appropriate.

With your reply we can take the next step.

Sincerely,

This sample is provided by Walter Nussbaum as a guideline, and is not intended for legal use.

Manufacturers' agents are by nature individualistic professionals who like doing things their way, be prepared to live with that. Some Principals attempt to impose sales policies customary for salaried employees, however that won't work. What's worse, the agent that agrees, thus fulfilling the manager's penchant for control, is likely an "easy money" rep. You eventually catch on, the relationship ends, huge amounts of your time and effort are lost.

Weigh your selections of agencies carefully. I've seen managers arbitrarily contract with reps just to fill in territory sales responsibilities and avoid the complex task of meticulously selecting them. A BIG mistake. Even with my first-class resume, if a manufacturer answered my response to an ad by immediately sending a contract to sign, I'd conclude they're just testing the water for a new product. I wouldn't expose myself, my time, my customers, or active DPB's to test-run widgets. It's fine to test-run a new product with existing reps, but seeking new agents to test-run a product would normally involve an agreed cash draw.

Building a successful rep network takes dedication and persistence. The cost of a trial-and-error approach will diminish your overall success. The cliché: "Get it right the first time" was never more important than assigning reps to territories. Responsible, progressive reps will require a secure contract, and that's a good sign.

THE PERIPHERAL STUFF

let's not argue about this

Sales meetings help, but having one every year is too often. Some reps think even semiyearly is a burden. In my experience manufacturers rarely have sales meeting for agents. However, if you belong to trade organizations, their conferences offer sales meeting opportunities. I believe agents should pay their own expenses, except perhaps if the manufacturer calls a special gathering to introduce a new product. In that case the manufacturer should pick up hotel costs.

A manufacturer visiting the rep's territory is a good practice; however, arranging to travel with a rep should be a cooperative effort. Never force the issue. The rep must utilize this opportunity carefully. Sales managers, engineers, or owners who take a few days to travel with their reps on sales visits should also do so expeditiously. Expect appointments and curricula to be maximized. If agents are not so prepared, you're of little importance to them. Typically, the agent can use visits from plant personnel to harness an order that's been on the fence or see an engineer, purchasing agent, or contractor who's been reluctant to make a change.

Plant personnel visit can also open closed doors. There is another reason to make sales visits with agents: If you're suspicious of having an "easy money" rep, solicit a visit to their area. Check the rep's preparation. It's easy to tell if the sales visits you make together enhance ongoing new customer efforts of the agent or if your visits merely fill time with existing customers.

U.S. manufacturers that sell widgets made outside the U. S. as part of their product line, i.e., (the same widget but a larger size,) should communicate that fact to the prospective manufacturers' agent. An open disclosure of the manufacturer's contract with the foreign company would convince agents they are dealing with an ethical company. In fact, that would attract agents who are otherwise reluctant to consider arrangements with manufacturers who don't have production control of all their products. Agents know that serious delivery, communication, pricing, and engineering problems can develop, when companies go outside their own production to offer auxiliary items, especially those made overseas. Importers who are not manufacturers exacerbate the problem. I wouldn't become involved with an importer, nor would most agents. Weigh that issue carefully before you jeopardize a customer with an imported item. I'd go so far as to say, a manufacturer should not sell imported auxiliary widgets through agents without having solid, exclusive documents with your source. Documents so well implemented you can show them to a prospective agent. That openness will lock in the agent's trust.

If your company is an offshore manufacturer establishing your own office, manufacturing, or warehouse in the U.S., reps will be very interested in your products, because that category of manufacturers work especially well with manufacturers' agents.

Manufacturers that publish literature, generate leads, have classy websites, advertise, exhibit at trade shows, have an 800 number and other aids are coveted by reps. Necessary bookkeeping procedures, copies of correspondence, invoices, and an accounting of paid invoices with commission checks are basic requirements for agents. I've represented two companies that kept records of phone inquiries and passed them on to me; that's a first-class sales tool. I loved it, and the individuals I contacted were impressed that their factory query led to my follow-up.

Cooperation is a two-way street, but don't expect sales visit reports. However, do look for feedback on field service, and   important quotes; especially those sent to new prospects. Always!

DRAW A LINE IN THE CONCRETE

trust is a must, but sign on the line

The written agreement or contract is crucial; it's the backbone of the agent and manufacturer relationship. It usually defines exclusive territories by states or parts thereof with counties. I've signed one that divided areas by ZIP Codes, which made tracking paperwork less cumbersome, but more difficult to follow by map. Commission rates vary with product types and volume considerations. The following are a few examples: A capital investment sale i.e., (a large machine tool or road construction machinery,) might be 20%. High-volume screw machine parts sold in thousands to an OEM may be 5% or less. Machine shop services are in the neighborhood of 10%. Construction materials vary from 5 to 15%. Volume sliding scales are sometimes appropriate. Split commissions occur when purchasing, engineering (specifier) and shipping point fall in three different territories. Variations depend on the industry, but if overly detailed, can become a burden. An acceptable example might be: 50% commission for order territory, 25% for specifier or engineering, and 25% for shipping point. Just as often it's 33 1/3% for each. You know best who deserves the commission in your industry. It's wise to establish within your contract that you, the manufacturer, are arbitrator with final decisions on split commissions. That prerogative may be needed, if two agents claim engineering specification or other split sale circumstances occur.

Presenting an agent with a fair, exclusive agreement at the get-go is a big step in establishing trust in a Principal/Agent relationship. Sales management should be involved in drafting the agreement, so don't leave contracts completely to others. Read the MANA contract to see if you can use it, as is. Have your attorney examine and consider it, then change what the lawyer thinks is in your best interest. However, be careful, as your attorney may be biased when drafting an agreement for you, especially if the concept of manufacturers' agent is foreign to your attorney. That attorney's agreement could be one-sided unfairly favoring you, the manufacturer, and encumbered with shrouded legal jargon. Alternately, incorporate some of your attorney's document, then draft your own. Territory, commissions, split commissions, and other portions are often listed separately in an addendum of the contract. A simple, fair example that's part MANA, part segments from other contracts I've signed, and my own interpretation of an equitable agreement, can be found at the end of *Take A Manufacturers' Agent To Market*. I don't advocate using this example unless your attorney believes it's legally binding. Do your best to keep any resulting variation simple.

Using the buddy system and handshakes in place of formal written agreements won't work. Handshakes sure, but show me the document. *It's logical: Manufacturers' agents that insist on proper contracts are **obviously** planning to invest time and develop sales for your widget. Now, that distinct fact should convince you that fairly written contracts are in everyone's best interest.*

If you present a one-sided contract with hidden phrases that put a manufacturers' agent's company in jeopardy, you've sent up a red flag. Successful reps, who could build your company sales, will vanish. In all likelihood they will politely cut off communication. They have no reason to justify their stance, they'll just sign with your competitor. Stay away from unscrupulous agreements; *they attract* "easy money" reps who sign anything and take whatever commission comes their way. You won't develop your product with them.

Manufacturers that propose house accounts at the beginning of an arrangement will deter most agents, especially large rep companies, who won't hassle with them. Record-keeping is cumbersome, and if your house account restricts an agent from selling your product to one of their existing customers, it creates a perplexing situation. Early on I agreed to one or two house accounts that were rationally defensible. Depending on the product, house accounts can be arranged so they become a permanent part of the agent's territory after a prescribed period of time or when the agent's overall dollar volume reaches an agreed amount. However, I've known singular reps that won't touch contracts with house accounts.

Don't propose house accounts unless they represent substantial volume. Holding commissions of a few dollars is another red flag. "No thanks! They're Penny Ante," reps conclude, "that manufacturer isn't really committed to reps, they won't get my time." Therefore, though a house account might work in unusual circumstances, weigh the implications carefully. Don't lose a chance to sign a good manufacturers' agent by holding onto one house account. This is your call. The old adage, "You get what you pay for," comes into play.

After the details have been settled, it's customary for the manufacturer to mail two signed copies of the final approved contract to the manufacturers' agent.

The agent completes the manufacturer's copy by signing one and returning it to the manufacturer.

If there's a good part to a one-sided contract and the "easy money" rep they entice, it's this: Those involved, manufacturer and manufacturers' agents, get stuck in a whirlpool. They deceive, mistrust, then blame the other for their collective failure. Each attracts the other like a magnet, and it's good that they're together, it will keep them from contaminating the mainstream of growing successful relationships.

Here is likely the most poisonous development that can occur for a manufacturer. Don't unknowingly get caught; play it straight down the fairway. Follow through with the stipulations in your agreement; if you don't and the agent realizes you're violating it, that agent may *begin* just treading water, stop developing new business, and thereby *default* to an *"easy money" rep* without you knowing it. That situation can go on undetected for years. *If you get nothing else from this book, avoid policies that encourage an agent to default to the "easy money" rep posture.* Whew! I'm glad that bad stuff's over.

Something you might consider, but won't see in sample contracts is requiring the manufacturers' agent to complete an addendum you attach to the contract, asking they list their present Principals and the products those Principles manufacture. It's even more important, when you suspect a product crossover.

The fundamental premise of manufacturers' agents require they not represent one company whose product conflicts with another; that should be your game plan. If a partial conflict does exist, but you're anxious to sign a particular agent, verbally work out a mutually satisfactory arrangement that defines what products the agent will sell for whom or that all parties agree the rep determines which product best fits a customer's need at the time of a requirement. Thereafter, confirm that arrangement in writing.

Additionally, I recommend prior approval by the manufacturer for existing sub-reps as part of the contract. I also suggest a designation that future sub-reps cannot be appointed without the manufacturer's written approval; that's a must. *Sub-reps are a mistake.* You're better off making it clear that sub-reps are not acceptable.

A multi-rep agency may hire outside salespeople at their discretion, but be sure the agency defines territories per salesperson at the beginning of the relationship. Ask to meet new outside salespeople.

If through previous management's neglect you suspect some or all of your agents have defaulted to "easy money" reps, you have three ways to reestablish an outside sales presence. First, invest in salaried reps. Second, start over with new manufacturers' agents. Unfortunately you'll lose agents with product knowledge. Instead try a third option: Send your reps a letter along the lines of the following sample, one that demonstrates the attitude the letter suggests.

Sample Letter to Revitalize Existing Agents

Date

Dear Mr./Ms.
Company, address, etc.

It is time for a fresh start.

We are determined to succeed marketing our products through a network of manufacturers' agents and plan to aggressively solicit those agents whose other products enhance ours. Complementary, non-competing products are a necessity. This is not an ultimatum to our existing reps, but rather an offer to reestablish our relationship within a new, unbiased understanding. We pledge to reconstitute our efforts and abide by the principles of agent/manufacturer ethics. Our commitment includes territory exclusivity, which implies accurate and timely copies of all correspondence and invoices to agents. Agents will receive commission on all sales into the prescribed territory, regardless of how the sale is initiated. That last sentence should convince you we're serious.

In turn, we expect the same openness and cooperation from you, our representative. That begins with an updated principal list and (if the following applies) names of your employees now in the field, including any sub-reps.

We expect our reps to actively research for, discover, initiate, solicit, and develop new customers. *Mutual confidence* will be the primary objective in our agent/principal relationships. We have borrowed from Walter Nussbaum Jr's book, *Secrets From The Street*: "The better agents maintain existing accounts, the best open new ones."

Included is a new contract for your examination. Please respond in some manner within _____. We welcome dialogue at any time.

Sincerely,

This sample letter supplied by Walter Nussbaum Jr. and is not intended as a legal document.

TOO MUCH MUSTARD
RUINS THE BEANS

double-check your recipe

"Distributors and agents don't mix."
"Yes they do, but only if you stir well."
This situation requires careful planning and applies to those manufacturers whose products require utilizing agents and distributors. Territories that include distributors for after-market and/or OEM are acceptable within the confines of manufacturers' and agents agreements, as long as sales commissions are paid to agents in the area. Agents establish, oversee and assist the distributor and receive commission on distributor sales. Letters, invoice copies, and statements are handled with the rep in the normal manner. The genre of the marketplace will dictate discounts given by distributors to their customers, whether they are users, resellers, or OEM's. In some cases manufacturers of building products don't allow discounts for distributors, and price them at the same level as the contractor.

It can happen that a distributor located in one agent's territory can buy from the manufacturer, then direct ship into another agent's area. Customers could be after market, contractors, even OEM. But, and this is another BIG BUT, when the manufacturer issues an invoice to that distributor, the agent where the product is shipped (to the distributor's customer) gets part of a split commission. That agent is sent the same invoice copy the manufacturer sent to the agent where the selling distributor was located. The copied agent can (and logically will) alert the distributor/s, inside their area, and/or make contact with that customer themselves.

It's also a fact, if a distributor ships materials into another rep's territory from the distributor's own stock, no invoice record for that sale would exist from the manufacturer to alerts the agent into whose territory the material was sent. Therefore, distributor discounts allowed by the manufacturer control distributor selling to OEM's and other potential factory direct type customers. Distributor discount levels must always include margins that allow for an agent's commission. Consequently, to make a profit selling to direct factory type customers (OEM), distributors would be required to mark up their lowest price level, resulting in a higher price to the OEM customer than a direct factory purchase. That setup creates a level playing field.

However, sales to all other type users from a distributor's stock is up for grabs. Agents must appoint aggressive distributors in their areas that will compete with distributors in the territory next door. Agents must also be relentless with DPB's in their own areas. If agents discover an OEM in their area, or any company qualifying for direct factory purchases, buying widgets from a distributor's stock in another territory, it's easy to claim that customer by offering them direct factory OEM pricing. You can see how that system creates its own balance. *It's the agent's responsibility to be finding, and contacting direct factory qualifying customers (OEM) within their territory.* If they don't, then sales to an OEM at a *marked up price* from a distributors own stock can't be controlled and can legitimately occur in any territory.

It's clear distributors can't exist in territories with agents other than the prescription above. What's not so obvious is that distributors and manufacturers' agents can't operate separately in *different territories* for the same manufacturer. This rationale includes distributors in a territory, where agents don't tread. In other words, a manufacturer's marketing methods must include the normal agents commission consistent in all territories across the U.S., even if a territory is without an agent.

"Wait a minute," I've heard when explaining this situation, "That doesn't sound right." This is similar to THE OLD GOLFER SCENARIO. When utilizing manufacturers' agents, one must adjust old habits (thinking).

As we've seen, manufacturers' agents in separately defined territories work well; split commissions settle any territory sales and commission disputes. However, distributors by nature will sell a manufacturer's widget in any state, where it's possible. Owners of distributor companies in the northern states often find it necessary to make Florida sales visits in January.

The bottom line: Agents must have the ability to develop accounts over time, knowing that when a particular customer finally buys from the manufacturer, they will get commission. There can't be the slightest doubt, not a smidgen of a possibility. What happens when a distributor in a territory without an agent is allowed an additional discount equal to the missing agent's commission? That distributor then has the ability to sell from their own stock into any agent's territory at a price equal, or potentially less, than the factory prices quoted by agents. An agent's exclusive agreement is therewith useless. You can see why that won't work.

A definite no-no: Suggesting agents register companies they solicit creates a named-account basis.

Named account territories are unacceptable in the rep business, because they simply don't work. Tracking sales of named accounts is impossible, and the attempt is much too cumbersome for an agent's activity.

If you want a "Network of Agents" in the true sense, then agents must be confident that their daily effort produces commission when the manufacturer receives an order from their territory. With the correct program in place, companies, small and large, have grown rapidly marketing through manufacturers' agents.

BEAUTY IS IN THE EYE
OF THE BEHOLDER

be sure what you see is what you get

What qualities should be evident in an independent representative? First and foremost a willingness, even enthusiasm, to disclose the lines they carry or plan to carry. Checking it out may be as easy as visiting the agent's website.

Openness is a key attribute for agents and should include giving you a verbal marketing strategy for your product. Again, I'm not suggesting sales reports; that's not to be expected, but do ask about their industrial and commercial reference library. Ample, up-to-date manufacturers' directories and CD's are needed for research to find DPB's. Contractor sales agents should subscribe to a service for construction plans and bid schedules. If the agency doesn't have these tools, tread lightly, and know the reason why. Agents should have the resources to research and develop new customers for your product. Leads you provide are icing on the cake. It's also sound practice to *require* feedback to legitimate leads generated by you, the Principal. Reporting back to the manufacturer on important quotes to DPB's and customers should be the agent's practice. Ask the agency how they handle feedback in those circumstances.

I'll refrain from comments regarding age, except to say that an energetic attitude, regardless of age, is a must for manufacturers' agents. Does an attractive young saleswoman calling on a male purchasing agent or male contractor have an advantage over an aging, overweight man? In my opinion, it's only human that "everything else being equal," the woman calling on a male purchaser is likely to get the order. Yet, in some industries the good-old-boy network closes out women. My editor said, "Be careful writing about these issues; discrimination is a sensitive area." However, understand, "everything else being equal," is purely hypothetical. Salespeople don't all have the same charisma, smarts, and persistence. So look for those traits in your search for manufacturers' agents.

Remember, references from other Principals the agency represents can be convincing, if you're on the fence about signing an agent. The agency your considering should offer you a list of those companies with contact names. Take time to check them out.

Some prominent associations like CSI (Construction Specifiers Institute) offer certification for salespeople within their industry, a big plus when considering representatives. Agents that are MANA members are a strong positive.

Humans have an uncanny ability to sense another person's character. Marriages are based on natural attractions. To confirm a long-term intention, those relationships require a document, the marriage certificate. Agents and manufacturers need the same contract commitment. Living together works for individuals, because a physical and emotional attraction keep people together—well, at least half the time. With agent/manufacturer relationships, the product is the physical attraction and the contract must fulfill the emotional need.

Show Me The Money

motivational speeches, like black coffee, wear off

Commissions are the incentive. Motivational speeches are of no significance to a manufacturers' agent. *Excite them with money.* A Principal I represented made an offer to raise commissions from 7-1/2% to 10% for new customers that I added during an extended period of time. The higher rate would endure as long as those new customers did; it moved me and my other salespeople. Give the commission increase a try, but don't penny-ante agents with a marginal cutoff date that disqualifies a new account. Raising commission to add new customers worked so well for my manufacturer, the new account incentives became a permanent practice.

Cutting commissions on marginal quotes is a sore spot for reps. You'll need to anticipate where manufacturing costs create close margins and use a sliding commission scale. *Most important: Make rates, payment schedules, commission splits, or sliding commissions rates clear at the beginning of the relationship.* Commission rates should be printed prominently in the contract, usually within an addendum. Reps in the construction field are often encouraged to set their own commission at quoting time.

After an extended time and expense chasing an account, the agent expects full commission. Asking the rep to accept reduced commissions to secure a foothold at quoting time may seem reasonable to the manufacturer, but not to the agent. Remember, an agent may have inside information to guide the quotation, and you'll need their input.

As a manufacturer you may be able to shave 5% off overall production costs. Don't suggest you're willing to cut 5% from the price of each widget, if the agent will accept a 5% commission cut, thus, providing a 10% quote reduction. If the agent's commission rate is 10%, you're actually asking for a cut of 50%. Think of it this way: You ask a 10% agent to cut 5% commission from a quote, but they turn it around and ask you to cut 50%. "Ridiculous," you say, "With my overall costs I'll lose money."

"Exactly," the agent responds."

Again, I'll repeat: It's imperative that commission schedules are clearly stated in the contract at the offset.

Lastly, this suggestion will maximize communication within your company, and make an immeasurable difference. Create direct liaisons between management and manufacturers' agents, giving the agents direct access to top management (boss) within your company. Agents aren't likely to stop within the normal hierarchy when production errors or late delivery cause problems for their customers. If yours is a large company, *let key personnel know your reps have the option of communicating directly with the boss, manager, or owner.* When it's known that the manufacturers' agents have a open channel of communication to the boss, teamwork improves. Encouraging agents to copy the boss on certain types of e-mails to inside personnel might be prudent.

Now we come to my final justification why a manufacturer might consider independent manufacturers' agents as outside sales representatives in lieu of salaried salespeople. Weigh this! *Think of the impact in professional sports, if the athletes were paid only when they win a game. One wouldn't have to wait for the playoffs to see the best performances.* Point spreads would be based on results not hype.

Place your bets!

Agency/Principal Agreement

This agreement is made on the date shown below by and between.

Date:_____

_____**("Principal")**,

and _____**("Agent")**

1. Exclusive Representative. Principal grants to Agent the exclusive right (to the exclusion of Principal and all claiming under or through Principal), by acting as Principal's sales representative, to solicit orders for the Principal's goods, equipment and/or services ___**(See exhibit A)**___(Products) within the following geographical or otherwise defined area. _____**(See exhibit B)**_ ___(Territory). Agent agrees not to represent another manufacturer within the defined area whose product or service is directly competitive to Principal.

2. Sales Policy. The prices, and terms of sale (Sales Policies) shall be established by Principal. If possible, notice of Sales Policy changes shall be given by Principal to Agency 30 days prior to changes.

3. Orders and Collections. Orders for Products within the Agent's territory shall be subject to acceptance by Principal. The Principal agrees to refer and/or copy agent on all inquiries, and promptly furnish Agent with copies of all correspondence and pertinent documents between Principal and Customer. All invoices shall be rendered by Principal to Customer , with copies to Agent. Responsibility for collection rests with Principal,; however, Agent agrees to assist Principal with collection when appropriate.

4. Agent's commission. The commission payable to Agent on orders from the Agent's territory shall be deemed earned by agent upon acceptance or delivery of an order by Principal, whichever occurs first. Commission rates shall be _____**(See exhibit C)_____** (Commission Rate). Commission shall be computed on the net amount of the invoice exclusive of freight costs. A Split Commission percentage for a specification originating from one Agent's territory for shipment into another Agent's territory

will be determined as given in _____**(See exhibit D)**_____
(Commission Split). Full commission is paid to Specification Agent
(with information furnished by agent) when shipment is made into
a territory without another Agent. All commissions due agent for
sales in Agent's territory shall be paid on the 10th of the month,
immediately following Principal's receipt of payment from the
customer.

5. Relationship Created. Agent is not an employee of Principal,
but is an independent contractor, who shall have sole control of
the manner and means of performing under this agreement. All
expenses incurred by Agent by promoting Principal's goods
and/or services in connection with this agreement shall be borne
wholly and completely by Agent. Agent does not have any right,
power or authority to create any contract or obligation, either
expressed or implied on behalf of Principal.

6. Term. This agreement is for an initial period of 18 months and
shall automatically renew for successive 1-year periods. Following
the 18-month period, either party may terminate this agreement for
good cause by giving written notice via certified mail to the other.
The "Termination Date" shall become effective 90 days after
notice is given. If the agreement is terminated, all orders received
and accepted by Principal from Agent's territory prior to effective
date of termination will be due commission as given in Paragraph
Four regardless of when orders are shipped or invoices rendered.
Agent shall be entitled to receive full commission from quoted
projects that become orders within one year following effective
date of termination.

7. Hold Harmless. Principal shall save Agent harmless from and
against and indemnify Agent for all liability, loss, costs, expenses or
damages howsoever caused by reason of any product (whether or
not defective), or any act or omission of Principal, including but not
limited to any injury (whether to body or property) sustained by
any person or to property, and for infringement of any patent rights,
or third parties, and for any violation of municipal state or federal
laws or regulations governing their products or their sale. Agent
shall hold Principal Harmless from and against and indemnify
Principal from any loss, costs, expenses or damages incurred by
Agent fulfilling this agreement.

8. Notices. This agreement contains the full and final agreements between the parties, and becomes effective when signed by parties noted hereon. Any notice demand or request shall be in writing and deemed effective twenty-four hours after having been deposited in the United States mail, postage prepaid, registered or certified to the addressee at their main office. Any party may change their office address for purposes of this agreement by written notice in accordance herewith.

(Principal): _____

By: _____

Signature: _____

Date: _____

Principal's Address: _____

_____

(Agent): _____

By: _____

Signature: _____

Date: _____

Agent's Address: _____

_____

EXHIBIT A - PRODUCTS

EXHIBIT B - TERRITORY

EXHIBIT C - COMMISSION

EXHIBIT D - COMMISSION SPLIT

This sample is provided by Walter Nussbaum as a guideline and is not intended for legal use.

EPILOGUE

There are people within the manufacturing community whose self-respect guides their quest for money and success; my long career as a manufacturers' agent would not have endured without them. Empirically, no matter how you cut it, when trustworthy people come together, you've got an old-time business relationship—productive and profitable. I've been very fortunate to have such experiences. They are the most memorable parts of my business life. Thanks to you all!

ACRONYMS

AC	Alternating Current
CEO	Chief Executive Officer
CSI	Construction Specifiers Institute
DC	Direct Current
DPB	Definite Possibility of Business
FI	Forget It
ICBBS	Industrial and Commercial Business to Business Sales
MANA	Manufacturers' Agents National Association 6A Journey, Suite 200 Aliso Viego, CA 92656 Ph. 877-626-2776 Visit manaonline.org
OEM	Original Equipment Manufacturer
PA	Purchasing Agent
PO	Purchase Order
POVL	Put On Visit List
RFQ	Request For Quote
SIC	Standard Industrial Classification
SA	Script Analysis
Sub-rep	A manufacturers' agent/rep that has an agreement with another agent for part of the agent's territory (not recommended)
TA	Transactional Analysis
WFS	Water Fountain Syndrome